Searching for
Shangri-La

北京版权局著作权合同登记
图字 01-2008-1823 号

Searching for Shangri-La
by Laurence J. Brahm

First Edition 2008
Copyright by New World Press, Beijing, China

ISBN 978-7-80228-586-6

Published by
NEW WORLD PRESS
24 Baiwanzhuang Street, Beijing 100037, China

Distributed by
NEW WORLD PRESS
24 Baiwanzhuang Street, Beijing 100037, China
Tel: 86-10-68995968
Fax: 86-10-68998705
Website: www.newworld-press.com
E-mail: frank@nwp.com.cn

Printed in the People's Republic of China

Searching for
Shangri-La

Off the Beaten Track in Western China

Laurence J. Brahm

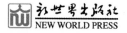
新世界出版社
NEW WORLD PRESS

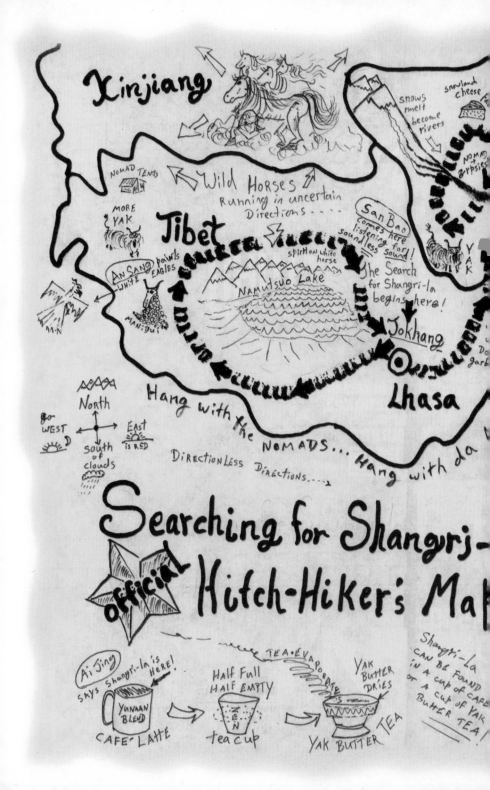

To Long Xiaolong (Khyentse Wangchung),

who grew up watching his father search for Shangri-La

Contents

YUNNAN 125

Questions, No Answers

Everyone asked me why I came to China, as if there was some fault, or some strange reason. Till today, they keep asking me this question. The truth is, I do not have an answer. So I used to make up answers.

As a student, I worked as a tour guide taking American tourists around China. They always asked me why I came to China. I told them I did not have an answer, so they gave me an answer. They would whisper among themselves that I must have been the child of missionaries. I said no. They did not believe me. After a while, I just told everyone that I was a child of missionaries.

Then I became a lawyer, a business advisor, a writer, a consultant, a commentator, and then everyone wanted my comments on everything related to China. After all the comments, press interviews, board meetings, and meetings with all those CEOs visiting China every year, the question would always come up again — "Why did I come to China?"

Again, I had no answer, but they insisted that there must be an answer. Everything must have an answer, otherwise the market economy will collapse. We will not be able to sell books that provide instant answers, or products that are the answer to all questions. There are religious books and videos, and multi-media packaging of the answers you need, but they are answers that you just have to pay for, credit card and you can pay over the

Internet, because it makes things so convenient. Do not tell me there is no answer. The answer must be in black and white, very clear, easily explained and capable of being packaged, franchised and distributed to all answer-seekers seeking answers to the same question.

I made up an answer for those who were curious, I told them that I came to China in 1981, inspired by Edgar Snow and Han Suyin, looking for Mao's China, and found Deng's China. When everyone in China was making too much money to talk about Mao anymore, I stayed. This answer was always acceptable, because in the minds of those hearing it, I must be staying in China to make money. This sounded acceptable and constituted a good answer. The truth is, I did not have an answer.

I still do not have an answer. Now I am tired of China as I have come to know it — everybody making money, thinking about money, talking about money and living for money in its pure cash accountable form. It seems like they all worship money now. Everyone is willing to sell everything in China for money, then sell what they buy to make more money. This is not the China I came to 22 years ago. This was not why I came to China.

Beijing today is no longer Beijing. The tree-lined streets no longer have trees, only cement. The old courtyard houses are gone, replaced by cement. There seems to be nothing here but traffic and cement. The city government is very proud of its cement because it looks just like the cement in America. They keep putting more cement on top of the cement, to try to make the city look more like America.

Everybody calls me to ask for advice on how to make money in China. I guess the Western businessmen have discovered that they can sell cement to China. My phone is always ringing, ringing, ringing, ringing, ringing, ringing, and still ringing. Sometimes, these businessmen who are calling me are upset that I have not read my e-mails. They expect me to wait for an e-mail, as if my life was embodied in an electronic device. I would rather wait for nothing at all. I tell them to stop sending me e-mails because I will not sit in front of a computer waiting for their e-mails, waiting to die looking and waiting and hoping to receive and send an e-mail. I cannot believe that life can be concentrated and reduced to one single digitized electronic message, which is not even spelled correctly.

They call me instead, and the ring, ring, ring, ring, ring, ring, ring of a mobile phone goes ringing through the pulse of my mind, for as long as I can stand the stress factor induced by the excessive talking. To solve the problem, I gave everybody my mobile phone number, then switched off the phone and bought another phone. This, however, did not solve the problem.

I began to ask myself the question: "What am I doing here? Why did I come to China?"

Then I had a dream. It came back to me every night. I had dreams of wild Tibetan ponies, white ponies running in uncertain directions. They were running across a vast Tibetan plain. It was surrounded by snow-capped mountains, but they could not reach the mountains. I was not certain which direction they were running in, but I knew it was uncertain. So I decided to follow the Tibetan ponies.

Uncertain Directions

Where is Shangri-La? Is it Tibet? Some tourists say that Qinghai has more of that Tibetan feeling than Tibet itself, as if foreigners can determine better than Tibetans themselves what Tibet should feel like. Some call this packaging.

The town of Lijiang, once an ancient kingdom in Yunnan, discovered a stone tablet with the Chinese characters "Xiang-ge-li-la" (Shangri-La) carved on the stone. So Lijiang advertised that it was Shangri-La. Tourists poured in. But another county called Zhongdian said that they were Shangri-La. Tourists started going there too. Then some people in Sichuan said that Shangri-La must be there too. They joined the dispute.

In fact, none of the officials in any of the self-proclaimed Shangri-La were looking for Shangri-La. They were just looking for tourist dollars on the back of packaging, franchising and distributing Shangri-La.

One day, I was having coffee with the pop singer, Ai Jing, at a Beijing Starbucks. "A café is like a peach garden beyond the realm," she explained. "If you want to find a place that is more expansive, well, everyone has this in their minds, a place where they can feel freedom from urban hassles." I began to think about this as I stared into a cup of café latte, looking for a connection to this peach garden thing.

I told her about the Tibetan ponies and my decision to follow

them even if the direction was uncertain. I described the place where I kept seeing the ponies, a vast Tibetan plain surrounded by snow-capped mountains. She said it sounded like Shangri-La, a place she had heard of once, or maybe twice. It could be found in a cup of café latte if one looked carefully enough. I looked into my cup of café latte and did not understand. She said I was not looking carefully enough.

The question is: how to find a new direction without breaking course with the direction that you have been going for such a long time? If you go in one direction long enough, it is easy to believe that this is the only direction or the right direction until you eventually run out of time. The only way to find a different course is to change the direction you have been going in. This may be done through definitive action, or inaction. To do this, you must stop everything you are doing and place them all in front of you like a deck of cards. Just spread them out in front of you, then wait for the wind to blow them away.

I told Ai Jing that I was heading west, in search of an uncertain direction, in search of Shangri-La. "You ought to try," she said. "People talk of Shangri-La, but there are many controversies over where it really is. If you want to search for it, I think it must be in the west. Take a road and follow it, just go without following any direction." She said that if I were to do this, I should hitchhike. This was the best way to travel in China because the direction would be uncertain and I would end up wherever I was dropped off. In such a case, when dropped off, I should just keep walking,

all by myself, in a certain direction. If uncertain, I could always ask for directions.

Conversation with a Yak Skull

I have watched you decompose.
I have seen eagles pick at your
sightless eyes and ants
suck marrow from your bones.

I have wandered to lost eries
where eagles die.
Only to find a talon
and a few feathers
rotting in the sun.

And there in eve-tide stillness
I watched my shadow linger,
stretch and dissolve into the night.
Where motionless upon a distant land
time ceased to be measured
and all but the sky
was soon forgotten.

Tibet

Asking for Directions

I left the airport. I began down the road toward Lhasa. I thought the search for Shangri-La should begin in Lhasa, but was not completely sure. So I started asking for directions.

It is said, upon arriving in Tibet, one should stop at a temple before entering Lhasa, But it is not said which temple to stop at or where one can find the particular temple. It is only said to be alongside the road. So I followed the road. Then I came to a temple. I did not know whether it was the right temple but went in anyways after asking the monks whether this was a temple. They said that there were many temples on the road to Lhasa. They asked me which one I was looking for.

I asked a monk for directions. He offered me yak butter tea. I stopped asking him for directions and drank the tea. It smelled of yak butter. The feeling was warm in the early Tibetan morning when the sky is still cool and one feels that earth has not yet entirely awoken. The monk explained to me that to search for directions, I should begin with a cup of yak butter tea.

I tried to explain that I was searching for a place called Shangri-La but was not sure which direction to go in. Should I continue traveling to Lhasa, or should I go somewhere else? The monks looked at me as if they understood an uncertainty in such a question which should not be answered with too much haste. They poured me another cup of yak butter tea. I drank it.

Entering the inner chamber, I found myself staring at the penetrating composure of White Tara, the Tibetan Bodhisattva of mercy and knowledge, with eyes on her hands, feet and forehead. She is said to see all, to know all. I stared at her eyes. She stared back with composure and sympathy. The room was consumed by the silence of burning incense — scent decomposing in flame. The silence of the incense was dissipated by the ring of a temple bell — the sound of which was dissipated by the ring of my mobile phone. An old friend was calling. It was Douglas Gerber calling from Hong Kong. A high-flying corporate executive with an American multinational corporation, Douglas was a quiet practitioner of Tibetan Buddhist meditation. He told me that his teacher, the Living Buddha Beru Khyentse Rimpoche, would be returning to Lhasa any day. He would probably be in Lhasa when I was.

Great! I would meet Rimpoche again after so many years. I asked Douglas when Rimpoche would arrive, where he would stay and when I could see him. I asked these questions with exactness. But Douglas did not know when Rimpoche would arrive or depart. Such details were unimportant, if I wished to see Rimpoche, I should look for him. Douglas gave me a couple of mobile telephone numbers of people who might know where Rimpoche would be. "Try calling the numbers," Douglas suggested. If I could not find the Living Buddha, I should not worry at all. The Buddha would find me.

I left the temple and hitchhiked down the road. The road passed a rock. There was a large Buddha carved on the rock, painted bright yellow and blue with a touch of green and red. White *hada* scarves and colored *jingfan* prayer flags fluttered in the wind where they had been placed.

You could see the statue from the road, but could not touch it unless you crossed the river. A young boy offered to lead me across the river. Placing his forehead against the hand of the statue he suggested that I do the same — ask for blessing and make a wish. I did so and made a wish. I asked the stone Buddha to help me find Shangri-La. The young boy asked for money.

A Cup of Yak Butter Tea

For Tibetans, the greatest pilgrimage is to Jokhang Temple (Da Zhao Si in Chinese), the origin of Tibetan Buddhist philosophy. The process of arrival at Jokhang is a journey. Tibetans prostrate themselves every step of the way. Hands clasped in prayer are placed on forehead, chest, and waist, falling on both hands and knees, face down upon earth, fingertips stretching and reaching forward. This is an act of ultimate submission to Buddha, Teachers, Bodhisattvas, and Guardians — in this order. Each prostration brings them only one step further to where their fingertips stopped, only to begin prostrating again. This is how the pilgrimage to Jokhang Temple begins and ends.

To prostrate repeatedly across the distance traveled on the journey to Jokhang Temple is an act of faith Tibetans live for and is a journey to be completed at least once in a lifetime. For some, this may require months of walking and prostrating; for others, years. On the plaza before Jokhang Temple, along the concentric roads winding around Jokhang Temple, one can see many Tibetans prostrating. Some have traveled long distances, others entire lifetimes.

So for me, the search for Shangri-La began at Jokhang Temple. This was the logical place to begin such a search. Here, more than 700 years ago, during the height of the Tang Dynasty, Emperor Tang Taizhong presented Princess Wen Cheng to the Tibetan king, Songtsen Gampo, as an act of unity between two peoples. She brought with her a statue of Sakamuni, the first Buddha. The temple was built around this statue.

Around the temple, concentric rings of roads unwind, lined with enormous brass Tibetan prayer wheels. There are prayers written and tucked inside the wheels. If you turn them, it is likened to saying the prayers, in this manner, the temple is always surrounded by the whirling energy emitted from the concentric turning of wheels. Pilgrims coming to the temple must follow the cyclic path and turn all the wheels. You can turn them clockwise, but not counter-clockwise. Clocks cannot be turned backwards.

It is said that Princess Wen Cheng brought Buddhism to Tibet and that she smiled (but remembered not to laugh) like the Bodhisattva, Guan Yin. Jokhang became a center of learning; a center for the spread of Buddhist philosophy, from here, the philosophy of the ideal Shambhala, or "Shangri-La" extended to Nepal, Bhutan, Qinghai, Yunnan and eventually, throughout the world. So logically, the search for Shangri-La should begin at Jokhang Temple. I was to learn by coming to Jokhang Temple that to begin such a search, one must begin by disengaging from the logical.

Such disengagement began when I entered the heavy red gate of Jokhang Temple, smothered in the smell of incense and yak butter oil. I entered the door and crawled up a narrow staircase to the rooftop looking for Nyima Tsering, one of the 99 monks who administer Jokhang Temple. I found him in a room and he offered me yak butter tea. I began to look for Shangri-La in the cup of tea, and remembered to look carefully. I was not looking carefully enough.

Nyima Tsering complained about the tourists. There were too many of them. While on one hand, he was pleased that so many people wanted to come to Jokhang to gain knowledge in Tibetan Buddhist philosophy. On the other hand, he was disturbed by the number of cigarette butts and Kodak film cartons being left behind. Due to the overwhelming international popularity of Tibetan philosophy and Shangri-La searching chic, the monks were now too busy sweeping up cigarette butts and used film cartons to have time for meditation, he complained. This was becoming a problem, interfering with the process of concentration. How could monks teach Buddhist philosophy to visitors seeking answers to their questions when the monks were so busy cleaning up the garbage they had left behind?

I stopped looking for Shangri-La to discuss this problem, hoping to provide him with an answer. Instead, Nyima Tsering brought me to the rooftop of Jokhang Temple to talk about Buddhist philosophy, while still complaining about the extensive littering. I left the yak butter tea, still hot, in his room. Eventually, the tea would evaporate. Yak butter, however, would remain.

"But now this is a problem," explained Nyima Tsering, waving his hands excitedly from under his saffron robe. "I feel both happy and sad. I am happy that so many people want to understand our culture through Jokhang Temple. On the other hand, I worry that

we have too many visitors. People come to Tibet with great hope of seeking Buddhist truths. However, upon arrival, they cannot obtain what they want. As Buddhist monks, we cannot introduce them properly to Buddhist Dharma, because there are many ideas, which we monks, including myself, do not have time to understand. One thing is, we need a quiet environment, a long time to meditate. This is a prerequisite. But there is also a requirement in Buddhism to save others' lives, which means we have to save all things with life. But before instructing others, we should instruct ourselves. It is not enough to only have a splendid temple filled with monks wearing these clothes," he pointed to his saffron robe. "The most important question is, there should be masters and teachers inside the temples too!" He was frustrated that most of the monks are spending their time administering crowds visiting the temple, instead of meditating or cultivating the principles they should teach.

"But people are coming here because this temple is said to be the root of Tibetan Buddhism," I asked. "So they're coming to the origin, right?"

"The origin of Buddhism is India," Nyima Tsering corrected me sharply. "However, it is a pity that Buddhism is now almost non-existent there because of past conditions, or maybe it's destiny. Maybe it did not establish very solid roots there. Or maybe there were too many battles. Today, we have to admit that the seeds of Shangri-La were only planted in the Qinghai-Tibetan Plateau when Buddhism arrived. They sprouted, bloomed, and fruited here. So I appreciate the vision of earlier generations, including King

Songsten Gampo. They transformed Indian Buddhism into Tibetan Buddhism by combining its principles with our environment, culture, and customs. So we should feel thankful to our ancestors. But right now, we have a new sense of urgency, as we, their grandchildren inheriting it, should be responsible for protecting Shangri-La. This is a big, urgent problem. If lost, it will not only be a loss for the Tibetans, but also a loss for the whole world."

"Are many people coming to Jokhang Temple in search of Shangri-La?" I asked.

"Many, many. Last week, I received many people from abroad. They told me once they set foot on Lhasa, they felt completely calm and comforted, and found things that they had lost. However, once they return to their homes, they become busy as time constraints pollute their hearts and souls again. No matter how much more money they have, regardless of how big their factories are, they cannot achieve real happiness. I think this is the power of Tibetan Buddhist philosophy. We may not have money, but we have the pride of knowing that our hearts are free and at ease. In the era of my grandparents, life was poor, but relationships between people were much better. Really, there are two aspects to being happy. One is your material well-being, the other is an open and free heart that is without restrictions. Without this, the happiness of a human being is no different from an animal. If we only have material things, or if you only have a beautiful home, a big factory, then it is like raising pigs. Pigs are fed only to be killed."

I was perplexed by the analogy. "So when somebody comes to

Jokhang Temple searching for Shangri-La, what do you tell them?"

"If you want to look for Shangri-La, remember that the real freedom of a human being is found in the heart and the soul. Racing in the process for economic development, we build factories and modernize technology. In the race for money, we lose our human nature and polluted our morality. Now the question is: How to seek and restore them? This is not only a question of my people, but also of people throughout the world right now. Many people have a good family and enough money to last several generations, but still, they do not feel happy. Why? Because it did not bring them more happiness. Rather, it brought them many frustrations. Therefore, balance is missing. Economy, industry and Western modernization are not enough. If we lose the human side of our world, in the end, we will still have to find Shangri-La and bring it back."

"But is it really about to be completely lost?"

"If you ruin or pollute Shangri-La, no matter how much money you have, you cannot buy the real thing back. It is a pity." Nyima Tsering shrugged under his robes. "People visiting Jokhang Temple are seeking inspiration, seeking Shangri-La. They should find more ways to purify themselves. You feel comfortable when you come to Jokhang Temple, but when you go back, you lose this feeling. It is only a temporary effect. The real effect depends on an understanding of yourself. Look for it from within and find the correct way to behave. I believe you do not need to come to Jokhang Temple, neither do you need to come to Tibet. In your hometown, whether it is in America, Europe, or any other country you can find it. There is no restriction of nationality, borders and time."

Nyima Tsering then began to connect lifestyle with environment. "In Buddhism, all lives are connected, including the ants, which are tiny. The best way of protecting the environment is through rebirth. For example, now I have an opportunity to become rich, to become a high-ranking official. Out of the unexpected, I can start enjoying life, but I will reject it, because I have a life to come back to. In order to become happy in the long run in my next life, I cannot accept this instant happiness blindly, which is not good for the future. As an example, a big weakness of our world is that the second life is not being acknowledged. Only one life, so I have to grasp this opportunity; if not, after I die, I would not have any opportunity to enjoy life. So they ride roughshod to destroy this environment, and built so many factories to pollute it. This is a criminal behavior. No matter how well-developed your economy is, your environment cannot compare with Shangri-La."

"The search for Shangri-La has brought me here, to Tibet." I asked, "Is this where I should come in search of Shangri-La?"

"I think Shangri-La is in Tibet," Nyima Tsering responded after a long pause. He seemed to be thinking about the question, pondering. "Why? Today we say the Qinghai-Tibetan Plateau is the last piece of clean land of humanity. Why? Because when my grandparents had the opportunity to ruin the environment, they said to themselves, 'No, we will come back to this world; we will, once again, live in this world — our mother — so we should not hurt our mother.' So I feel the Buddhist concept of re-incarnation is closely associated with the environment, the importance of protecting even the smallest forms of life in our eco-system. If we do not protect these cycles of life, then I think Shangri-La will disappear soon. In Buddhist teachings, there is no nationality. We are one family and the earth is our mother. Even the little ants are our brothers and sisters. This makes the world interesting and meaningful. Although with all those many factories and airplanes that bring us convenience, you will find yourself even further away from the real Shangri-La. You cannot find Shangri-La by looking down from an airplane. You can only find it through your own self and behavior."

"So you're saying that the destruction of our environment is now threatening Shangri-La?"

"Yes, natural resources must be used in a reasonable way," Nyima Tsering explained.

"We want to survive, and this is a prerequisite. Tibetan Buddhism has a weakness in that it allows for the eating of meat, though this is forbidden in Buddhism. Why? Our Qinghai-Tibetan Plateau is at a high altitude. Here, it is cold and lacks oxygen. The people are nomadic. Although killing is forbidden in Buddhism, human beings are more valuable. In order to survive on the Qinghai-Tibetan Plateau, it is permissible to kill some small lives. But in the end, you should repay the killing. But multinational corporations now ride roughshod to expand, damaging the earth in the process. To satisfy their desires, they destroy mother earth in the name of competition. There will be a time when the resources will be gone and what life can get from earth will become lesser and lesser. Therefore Buddhism can project very far into the future. To survive in this world, one should not seek too much luxury. Why? Life is reincarnated. We must also consider the future generations as they too must live on this earth. Despite all the scientific development and fancy technology, we cannot live on the moon or the sun. If you pollute this earth, it will be very dangerous for the future of humanity. People should rationally calm down to think, to seek, to reconsider. Our ancestors might have been very poor, but I feel in some ways, they were also very rich. They had a better environment and more resources, so perhaps they were richer than us. That is why I say we should think long-term. Scientists use microscopes, but cannot see the future. Buddha has bright eyes and can see very far. He is responsible for all living beings. We must be responsible for our own earth."

"So Shangri-La may be lost as we search for it," I thought out loud. According to Nyima Tsering, Shangri-La is not a place, but a cycle of our eco-system, a state of mind. "Was I right to begin the search for Shangri-La by coming to Lhasa?" I asked him.

"Coming to Lhasa to take a look is correct. To come to feel is right. Human nature is to explore. But most importantly, you should explore your own Shangri-La in your heart. This Shangri-La is forever and unlimited. But our universal earth mother is limited, so in Buddhism, we say the real hero is not to triumph over nature or our environment. The real hero is to triumph over our own frustrations, the things that blind your search for Shangri-La. Selfish stupidity, unknown in Buddhism, is of very short-term benefit. In the end, there is nothing, except increased frustration and pressure on your psychology. I have money, I have factory, but I am not happy. Even the beggars are more relaxed than me. This is the search for Shangri-La."

Staring up at the pure blue sky stretching like endless sea above us to the distant mountains behind Potala Palace, I thought about what Nyima Tsering said. I was lost somewhere between the blue sky and the mountains when Nyima Tsering's voice cut clear between the blue.

"You can experience Shangri-La here. However, the real Shangri-La is not only found in Jokhang Temple. No matter where you go, there is no map of Shangri-La that shows you which route to take to get there. So I will tell you the way. Do not defeat outside enemies, instead, defeat the enemy within yourself — selfishness. Eventually, Shangri-La can be found in your heart. It is not in Tibet, nor anywhere else. It is unfair to say this place is more Shangri-La than another, because ultimately, finding Shangri-La will depend solely on your own effort. Shangri-La cannot be obtained by weapons, science or troops. The further you seek your Shangri-La, the further away you will be. You can search for it forever. We should use non-violence, kindness, wisdom and reason to look for our Shangri-La, which is also called 'spiritual civilization' nowadays. You want to find the real Shangri-La? Look around you. I feel our world is a heaven. The hell in Buddhism is not created by God, but by yourself. Your own heaven or hell is all associated with your behavior. If human nature improves, the search for Shangri-La will become nearer."

Nyima Tsering then told me that the Living Buddha of Jokhang Temple was locked in meditation, refusing to see anyone at all. But there might be a chance he would see me. Nyima Tsering led me across the rooftop of Jokhang, winding from one level to another, around a corner, twisting in one direction, then another, across a small gallery and into a tiny room. He indicated I should kneel on the ground, present the Living Buddha with a white *hada*, and ask one or maybe two questions.

Sitting cross-legged was the Living Buddha of Jokhang Temple, a frail man with long thin white hairs on his eyebrows. Smiling as I entered the tiny chamber, he put down a long, thin Buddhist text he was studying on a small table before him. Reaching over and placing both hands on each of my arms, he touched his forehead against mine. He knew I had come with many questions. Before I could ask, I listened.

"Today I am 85 years old and have researched many religions in my lifetime, discovering that the greatest rationale can be found in Buddhism," explained the Living Buddha in a soft voice as he sat alone on a raised Tibetan bed with prayer scriptures laid before him, neatly yet somewhat scattered. "Through studying, I have discovered that to be pure is rational and very good. We must thank generations before us for bringing Buddhism to Tibet, and it was their greatest contribution. One generation after another brought

Buddhism here from India with an enlightened understanding and realization. This has served a great purpose. But in those days, there was a discrepancy, being that Buddhism only circulated within the realm of Tibet and not beyond. But it is said that many lamas are now disseminating Tibetan Buddhism throughout the world and this is of great purpose. I have heard that more and more people overseas are becoming interested in the notion of Shangri-La. This is the work and contribution of the great teachers. But it is only after a Buddha has attained enlightenment through correct study and bringing the enlightened way to others can one truly find the real Shangri-La."

"Is this why we have such a spread of Tibetan Buddhism overseas? It has almost become a fad." I was now on my second question.

"There are many overseas Tibetan Buddhist missionaries, but not all are real. Some are fakes. Therefore, one must be careful in searching for Shangri-La. It is not true that all Tibetan Buddhism is pure. Some things are being understood blindly without responsibility. It is best to go into the temple and study for twenty or thirty years, and this will give one great benefits. Only in this way can enlightenment be released. This is the true premise for searching for Shangri-La. Otherwise, you will blindly look for it but this is not necessarily a good thing. I hope you can find it. Approach this deeply, go further."

"Go further? How? What road to take?" Two and a half questions did not count as three.

Nyima Tsering blinked as the Living Buddha spoke.

"You must find the correct road and this is most crucial. Buddhism has created many different schools. You must be careful. Not all the schools are good. In the world, there are many religions, but some are blind faiths. At the same time, there are also many Buddhist schools where people follow blindly, where incorrect explanations are given. Such schools are useless. Sakamuni's words are clear and rational. Believers cannot blindly believe words that are repeated at any time. What words are of use to you and what words are not? Those which are useless should be thrown away. Those which are worthwhile should be used. Do not believe blindly. Separate the good from the bad. This is a question of principle."

Leaving the meditation chamber of the Living Buddha, I squinted in the sharp Tibetan sun. It cast shadows across the white rooftop of Jokhang Temple. The sun shifted position. The shadows grew into long thin lines, like a Dali painting. Stretching into infinity, they shifted. I watched the lines, and the sun. I squinted. They shifted. Then I thought about searching for Shangri-La in a cup of tea. I went back to Nyima Tsering's chamber, looking for the cup of yak butter tea I had been drinking that morning. Sure enough, I found the cup where it was left. It was partly, but not completely empty. It was full of yak butter, but no tea. The tea had evaporated. The yak butter had already dried.

Cold Thin Air

At 4:30 am, Tibetan air was thin and cold. This made climbing up a mountain in the dark difficult. Some people did not understand why one would want to climb a Tibetan mountain in the dark. It was like blindfolding oneself in a room and turning around in concentric circles to the point of dizziness. Such behavior was irrational and unexpected. It exceeded realms of the precise. It lacked a particular answer.

I climbed the mountain. The silence of morning darkness was broken by the trickles of a running stream. I stopped for a drink and remembered to listen for a moment to the trickles. It was the sound of water becoming round for the first time upon touching the body of a rock. It would never appear in this shape again after leaving the rock.

The patter of soft feet surrounded me. It was the sound of Tibetans traveling from distant places to climb the mountain. They were young and old and one of them was an old, crippled woman. She supported herself on two sticks, her back bent over. She climbed the mountain like a deer. With a smile which lit the wrinkles on her face, she offered to show me the way.

They came once a year. They climbed only in the dark before sunrise evaporated darkness. I followed them through the darkness. Following someone else was the only way to find a way up the mountain, so I had to follow. There was no time to ask for

directions. For them, this was pilgrimage and directions should not be asked. I followed them through a compact time span of thin Tibetan air. It tasted cold.

The Shoton Yogurt Festival occurs toward the summer's end, the best season for making yogurt, a critical sustenance for the Tibetans. It is a time of thanksgiving before the arrival of winter snows, it is a point in the transition of seasons when one may find a moment of introspection, a time to think about why one passes from one season to another with such ease, without paying attention to why.

The festival begins with pilgrimages to temples that are built on the mountains. Inside these temples, great *thankas* are kept. Upon the *thanka* canvasses are enormous paintings of the Buddha, Sakamuni. The *thankas* are so huge that they may be spread across the surface of a mountain. Once a year, in the early morning, over a hundred monks will be lost in chants and drones of Tibetan horns. They will lift the great *thanka* upon their shoulders to the height of a mountain and unroll it seconds before sunrise so that the first rays of light may touch the Buddha's face, so he may face the first rays of the sun for just a second before they roll up the *thanka* and put it away until the following year.

Colored papers representing elemental colors of life are shredded and tossed upon the Buddha's face together with offerings of white *hada* scarves, and even money. Tibetan pilgrims crouch before the vast *thanka*, touching their heads on it for blessings. Great chunks of turquoise embedded in brass or gold fittings braided into the hair of Kampa women touch the foot of Buddha. They press their heads to the vast *thanka* in prayers. They press the foreheads of their children and babies to the vast *thanka* for blessings. The lamas touch the pilgrims, who have been waiting patiently, with their yellow hats, giving them their blessings.

As the sun rises, the mountain is no longer shrouded in darkness. The early sunrays touch the Buddha's eyes, before which colored papers are tossed into a kaleidoscope of thin cold air which has now become a little warm. A mountain covered with the face of Buddha is overwhelmed by the prayers of the Tibetan pilgrims. The sound of the Tibetan long horns droning over chants of a hundred monks before golden temple rooftops and pagodas, touching air that is the space of the eagles. Hallucinated by the smell of pine incense kindling in earthen burners, they dance in the wind. They do not care much that prayers are said and blessings received or that moments are transitions of seasons. They forget that air is thin and often cold.

Soundless Sound

I met San Bao at Drepung Monastery, during the unfolding of the great *thanka*. In his own way, San Bao was searching for inspiration for new music. Recognized as one of China's greatest music composers today, from classical to pop, San Bao has created stars through his song writing and composition by writing hits for pop singers and movie directors like Zhang Yimou and Feng Xiaogang. I had seen him at a concert in Beijing, conducting an

orchestra that was playing his compositions. I had listened to his music and felt his compassion. I did not expect, however, that of all places, I would meet San Bao here in Tibet. Some might call this karma.

San Bao is actually ethnic Mongolian. The Mongolian people also practice Tibetan Buddhism. Lifestyle in the mountains and on the grasslands are similar to the Tibetans, so is their nomadic spirit. One afternoon, we sat together on the rooftop of Jokhang Temple, drinking yak butter tea. Potala Palace was within the distance and the crystal blue sky created an illusion that one could actually reach out and touch it. I tried to touch it, only to realize it was just an illusion, a distortion of perceptions. I began questioning my own perception of distance, space, time and music. We talked about sound.

"Your name 'San Bao' means 'three treasures'. It's a concept in Tibetan Buddhism, right?"

"This is my family name. As I am the third brother, so my family called me 'San Bao', or 'third treasure'. San Bao is directly related to Buddhism. I do know that. There is a San Bao Temple, but the specifics of this place are not known to me. I believe in reincarnation. Everything does not have a conclusion. When one thing concludes, a new one begins. A person's life is forever faced with making choices which require sacrifices. The gain from one's choice is also one's loss."

"Many people come to Tibet for inspiration," I wondered. "But why are we really here? What do you make of it?"

"Every person has a Shangri-La in his mind," San Bao explained. "Every person is searching for this. But people have their own individual viewpoints, and they will use their own familiar way to find their own dream."

"So is this search for Shangri-La the driving force behind New Age music, like the band Enigma?"

"From the music perspective, in the early 1980s, so-called New Age or World music emerged, reaching for the roots of ethnic elements and fusing them into modern lifestyle rhythm, creating pure sounds. From this point onwards," San Bao explained, "a variety of diverse New Age music forms sprang upon the scene. Many DJs and record engineers compiled and recomposed raw and ethnic sounds. Step by step, a new epoch of music emerged. I feel that other cultural forms are also following this pattern, creating a kind of 'crossover' movement. Collectively, the past twenty years may be viewed in retrospect as representing an epoch characterized by a search for the pure and the natural. You see, music has many levels of comprehension. For instance, New Age music has now become a fashion. Suddenly, it appears that everyone is doing this and it is now becoming overdone. Every person thinks that as long as you get some primitive sounds and patch them together, you have the New Age sound. For example, here in Lhasa, I saw a lama standing under a China Mobile advertisement, talking on a mobile phone. You will feel it is strange and a bit overstated."

"Through New Age music, do you feel that composers and songwriters are looking for something natural in ethnic sounds which they feel is missing in modern urban life today?"

"Missing something?" San Bao asked himself out loud, looking up at the pure blue sky, where waves of white clouds scattered in a distant illusion gave a sense of proximity. "What are we all missing? Nobody can really answer this clearly. In reality, Shangri-La represents a state of composure. Regardless of where Shangri-La might be, this is really not so important. It is a lifestyle, a state of composure, or the ideal in one's imagination." The clouds shifted, exposing more blue.

"Does this then represent an escape from the modern urban yuppie utopia?" I asked.

"People living in cities for long periods can find themselves short of inspiration. But every person's inspiration is different. Sometimes, I really want to go to some place which is far from the city, far from noise, maybe somewhere in the countryside or somewhere where there are no people. Just close the door and stay alone by myself without anyone around. I am a person who has an extreme dislike of cities. I do not like any city at all. I do not know why. I have a feeling of special admiration for those artists, such as painters. If I were a painter, I would certainly not live in the city because art can be completed by a person alone. But for me, this is not the case. To be a music composer, I must work with songwriters, musicians and recording engineers, because my work requires many people to be involved collectively to complete. Qian Zhongshu once said, 'City people want to leave the city. Country people want to enter the city.' Regardless of career or marriage,

people are just that way. I lived in this atmosphere and situation. So what I want is something different. In fact, however you look at it, it is just the same."

"The same, as compared to what?" I was more confused. "Can you give me an example of what you mean?"

"Once, I went to Yunnan," San Bao explained. "A friend there interviewed many people in rural villages, recording their lifestyles. He saw a local girl, who looked very open and expressive, so he wanted to interview her. After talking for a while, he fixed a time for the interview. At the time he spoke, the girl was wearing traditional ethnic clothes, with a lot of character, very interesting. The next day, when the village girl came for the interview, she did not wear her ethnic clothes, but rather, a modern dress with stylish shoes. Of course, this girl must have felt that she was dressed quite attractively. This shows a gap in culture. It is in fact very simple. It makes you really wonder. What is beautiful?"

"So is this why you came to Tibet? What inspired you most here?"

"Yesterday, I drove to *Namutsuo* Lake. It is a beautiful lake. But the local nomads will probably ask you why you would bother driving a jeep for such a long distance just to see a lake. They see this lake every day and do not see anything special there. The road to *Namutsuo* Lake evoked a feeling of traveling on a rough uncertain road. But then, suddenly coming over the hill, I saw the lake. It reminded me of the time when I was driving a car in the U.S.A., when suddenly I saw a city of neon lights appear in the desert, and that's Las Vegas. Back then, I also had this same feeling. Of course, both cases are two extremes of the same thing, but both situations created a feeling of awe after apprehension."

"Experiencing awe after apprehension ... maybe this is the search for Shangri-La. What do you think?"

"Many people search. This is just idealistic. The real dream is inside our own minds if your heart can really find it. I like to go to really rural areas where life is simple. In fact, it is not the place that I go to that is important, it is the process of getting there. People in the city, however, often do not even have the time to consider this single question. Many workaholics probably do not even think that this is Shangri-La. But I am not a workaholic. So people often ask me as if I am strange, whether I feel bored going off to that kind of place, working alone for over a dozen hours at a time? I say, maybe it is boring for you, but every person is different and has different feelings. Some people feel that if they have a nice house, a stable job in the city, a nice family and well-behaved children, then that is enough. They feel that that is their Shangri-La, their dream. Is there anything wrong with that? In fact, they live a real life and that is really great."

New world music and new lifestyle being fused with images and senses of the Qinghai-Tibetan Plateau, a lifestyle as far removed as one can get from that of urban yuppies seeking new world vision. The irony seemed striking. The question came back to what Nyima Tsering had said. Regardless of materialism, happiness was something you create with your own lifestyle and your own means.

Maybe this explained the rising international popularity of New Age music. I asked San Bao, "Then isn't any kind of ethnic music entirely inter-related with lifestyle?"

"Mongolian and Tibetan nomad music is completely integrated with the landscape," he explained, pointing to a Mongolian yak hair standard propped on one rooftop of Jokhang. Integrated lifestyle of these two nomadic peoples had made this Mongolian symbol of power Tibetan as well. "On the vast grasslands, there are actually very few people. Their lifestyle is focused on raising sheep and yaks. Sometimes, there is only one person out there with the sheep and yaks. Imagine, alone all day on the grasslands with nobody to talk to. So the nomad will sing. The space is too vast. Anybody who comes to such a place will feel its expansiveness as they cannot see anyone on the horizon. So what do you feel, what do you really want to do? Just scream out. Here you have the feeling that you can let yourself go altogether. Here, one's relationship with the forces of nature is the most basic. You can hear such a person sing from a very great distance. Completely alone, one will tend to sing to oneself just to make oneself happy. It is a pure relationship between an individual and the environment."

The day before, I noticed San Bao using a video camera to film two dogs sleeping in front of Jokhang Temple. I was really curious why he had bothered to film the dogs when so many other things were happening there. Before Jokhang Temple, Tibetans from all parts of the plateau, and monks from throughout the world, came to prostrate themselves before the temple doors. Hundreds of prayer wheels turned, circulating a powerful energy. Pine incense infused the temple plaza in a shrouded mysterious air. Visitors from every part of China and every country in the world came and went, purchasing Tibetan antiques and crafts in the surrounding market. With all of these comings and goings, I was very curious why San Bao chose to film two sleeping dogs. So I asked him.

"There were two dogs sleeping there. I filmed them because they had life. They slept there while everything else was going on around them. That was just the point I was trying to capture. To them, things around them did not matter. They were not bothered by them. But many people come to this place seeking something that is difficult to attain. If they cannot attain what they have come to seek, they may not understand the reason why and feel it strange. I have always had this kind of desire, and during the course of searching for this desire, I have been afraid that there will be people who do not understand what I am thinking. For instance, if you do not get out of the house for several days, people will think you are strange, because you are different from others. If you are not together with a group of people, others will think you are strange because you are different. But if you are together with everybody, you will ultimately seek your individuality rather than be the same as others. But in fact, you are really afraid that you will be different from others. This is where the conflict lies. But at the same time, you must be different from all the others. Character is not something you can find. This comes from the road you have traveled and the things that have become a part of your mind. It is not something you can find or create; it is a natural expression. In fact, I doubt many people will actually go out and search for their own Shangri-La. Most will be just floating without direction or follow the others."

"Then has the search for Shangri-La become just a fashion, like New Age music or fusion lifestyle living?"

"Many people will just do what is in fashion," San Bao shrugged, "instead of really finding Shangri-La. For instance, the other day, a whole bunch of fashion models had used Jokhang Temple as a background for their modeling. Why? This is very superficial. Things like this disgust me and I cannot accept it. In fact, it is quite frightening if you think about it. Real things must be found from within yourself, not just in a place. It can't be found just because you have come to Lhasa. The spirit within you is the most important. A monk who wanders, begging in the street, is looking for something. In fact, he may have already found it. Since his childhood, he may have left home in search of this, and in fact, this search is Shangri-La. I feel if I want to search for my own Shangri-La, there is still time. When it is complete, and when I look back, there should be no regrets. I do not have anything worth regretting. This life, as long as I have lived, as long as it is worth it, then that is good."

"There is a Buddhist concept of a voiceless voice. Can you tell me about this soundless sound?"

"I once discussed this in detail with a Buddhist," San Bao replied. "The sound within Buddhism is the most sensitive and the most basic element of all things. You see, I am a composer, so I am very sensitive to sound. This point of Buddhism is very difficult to understand. When I was young, my teacher taught me something that changed the way I would ever think. 'You must remember,' he explained, 'within music, the point of silence is actually a part of the music.' My realization suddenly had greater clarity. These words have influenced my own understanding of music ever since."

"So for you, what does Shangri-La mean?"

"One should sometimes just think about what one is doing and consider whether it is worthwhile or not. I often ask myself, what is the meaning of all these — the things I am doing, music I am composing. In this question, there is a powerful conflict. I think there are a lot of other things I must still do. When I talk with friends, they say that when you reach a certain age and you have already accomplished many things, you will suddenly wonder and discover what you really have done and what you really want to do. My Shangri-La is my own lifestyle. My greatest objective in life is to find Shangri-La, and through my own work, it is my search to find and express Shangri-La. But after much effort, people say such work is not commercial enough. They worry about the market. Actually, I don't care about this. As long as I have created it, then that is alright."

As San Bao explained the vision of his music, I noticed the Mongolian yak hair standard protruding from one of the rooftops of Jokhang Temple, sharp against the blue of the sky. Golden rooftops with guardian dragons and laughing lions framed the Potala Palace in the distance, which seemed so close. We sat on the rooftop of Jokhang Temple all morning, discussing the search for a sound that could not be heard. The blue sky, which stretched behind San Bao, seemed so close that it could be touched at any moment. Just reach out and grab a cloud passing by. Such is an illusion perpetuated by the blue sky. Such was its clearness. Awareness undistorted. If the Tibetan sky were a sound, a chime would ring forever.

"You must remember ... within music, the point of silence is actually a part of the music."

Yak

The yak looks like a great American bison with the head of a water buffalo. His body is shaggy with fur that flows in a great long mane, giving the yak the composure of a horse. The yak is the most essential, basic element of sustenance for the Tibetans. They drink yak's milk and yak butter tea, eat yak yogurt and yak milk cheese, which can be dried and carried in yak leather bags on horseback for days at a time when nothing else can be eaten. They also eat the yak itself. Yak meat can be air dried or chopped fresh into fine pieces, wrapped into dumplings and boiled as delicacy. Yak oil is burned in lamps as offerings in temples or to light one's tent in the dark. Yak fur woven into a tent is home.

Yak is the single ultimate perpetuator of life for Tibetan nomads. So when a yak dies, a solemn moment arises. The Tibetan way is to take its skull and present it to a *manidui* stone altar or hang it over a doorway for protection. This way, the yak spirit is perpetuated or oversees a passage. A yak is remembered by praying to its skull. This is a good way to remember someone you care about, but have lost.

During the Yogurt Festival, yaks are beautifully decorated with *hada* on their horns and flowers in their fur, like little girls preparing for a date. Bright saddle blankets with images of lions and dragons are strapped to their backs. I asked one Tibetan nomad feasting at the Yogurt Festival, "Where is your yak?"

"This is my yak!" he declared, pointing to a shaggy hallucination of kaleidoscopic colors.

I stared at the colors swirling in concentric circles of tinkling bells. "How long did you take to decorate your yak?"

"It took me ten days to completely decorate my yak," he explained. "The five colors symbolize the elements we live with — water, fire, sky, earth, and stone. These elements are always with us."

I wondered how somebody must feel about their yaks in dressing them up and adorning them with beautiful colors, like they are daughters about to wed. So I asked the nomad how he felt about his yak. He told me he was in love with his yak. He had raised the yak when it was a calf. "The yak is always with my family. He is part of our family."

Tassels and bells hang everywhere from the mane, to the saddle, to the tail. The tingle of bells is crisp, cutting the Tibetan air with a clarity that feels like blue porcelain cracking against the endless chime of bells. I asked about the bells.

"The bells are for protection. They are antiques and their chime is sweet," explained the nomad. "They have been passed down in our family, from generation to generation. So when we hear the sound of the bells, we hear the same sound our father heard, likewise for our grandfather before him, and our great grandfather before him. Can you understand the chime of yak bells?"

In a nomad family, yaks will be born and will die, generation after generation. Family members will be born and will die, generation after generation. A generation of people and yaks will come and pass, but the bells will be the same. As the nomads wander, the bells will travel across valleys and mountains, across vast space and passages of time. The chime of bells will pass from generation to generation of both yaks and nomads. Yaks and nomads will come and go. Bells remain. Their chime can still be heard.

White Eagles

Yang Jin is a Tibetan who had moved to Beijing as a child. She cannot speak Tibetan anymore. She has the face of Guan Yin. This shocked me when I first met her. Yang Jin's eyebrows stretched in thin round curves and her eyes evoked compassion. Her cousin Ang Sang is a painter in Tibet. He paints her eyes. Yang Jin said I must find Ang Sang when I go to Lhasa, which I did. I found Ang Sang in a quiet house in an even quieter lane. As I stared at his painting of a thousand-hand-thousand-eye Guan Yin, I realized that I was staring at Yang Jin. I wanted to ask him about his paintings. So I began by asking Ang Sang about Yang Jin.

"Yang Jin went to Beijing," I asked. "She found a good life there. Have you ever thought about doing the same?"

"Beijing is the capital of China," Ang Sang explained. "From a materialist aspect, it is very nice. But in Lhasa, I can find a feeling that allows me to paint, and there are many things here I can feel. I just walk without a specific direction, just look around and see the things I want. Inspiration for my paintings comes from the things I see and feel every day, so I cannot leave them. If I leave this atmosphere, I will leave my inspiration. Therefore, I feel this is a very special place, a place of spirit. I will stay here until I die. As an artist, I could not find a better place to be than here. You see, every person has their own Buddha in them and every person has their own temple within. Mine is expressed through my paintings.

Therefore, in this place, I can paint the things inside my heart."

"You cannot leave here. Is it because you cannot leave Shangri-La?"

"Yes, you can say this. Lhasa, or Tibet, has not yet been destroyed. It is clean. Here, you can see and feel the force of religious inspiration. But in many places, many big cities, this cannot be seen because it has been destroyed. Construction destroys much. In Tibet, you can still see people whose faces are pure and innocent. From inside a person, you can feel that person's value. So I will definitely stay here."

"Can you explain how you fuse tradition with modernity in your painting?" I asked.

"As soon as I went to Tibet University, I began to study the painting of traditional *thanka*. This is the most delicate and unique painting style of our people. But I cannot just take traditional painting and repaint it, as my own art is modern. So what I try to do is to fuse the most traditional elements of Tibetan life with my ideas to create modern art."

Ang Sang's paintings expressed a sense of solemn power through recurring images of Tibetan women covered in turquoise, the thousands of hands and eyes, and the unrestrained energy of white eagles (vultures). "Can you explain why you have so many white eagles in your paintings?" I asked.

"Once, I read about Tibetan sky funerals," he explained. "I was very touched. Buddhism is a person's purity and is an ultimate contribution. A Tibetan sky funeral is the final contribution of a person. You present the flesh of your body to the white eagles and they bring your flesh to the temples of heaven. Death becomes an event of life which exceeds reality. So many of my paintings have images of white eagles that bring you to another realm. This feeling reminds one that death brings you to the heavenly realm. Tibetans believe that only the white eagles can really bring your flesh to heaven. So I paint only white eagles. This is a part of human culture. Many of my works express something I feel within. My paintings reflect many feelings and inspirations that arise from real things and real feelings within. The white eagles of my paintings reflect Tibetan Buddhism. In Tibet, there are white eagles and they encircle an altar where the corpses are presented to the white eagles. The priests who cut the bodies to prepare them to feed the white eagles recognize them and can even call them by their names. Moreover, a white eagle's carcass cannot be found on the ground because when they die, they fly to heaven, it is all very clean, it is like we are transposed to heaven."

"Where can we go to watch the white eagles?"

"In Lhasa and in Ali, there are many places which have altars for presenting corpses to the white eagles. I went to Ali once and found many spirit mountains along the way. I remembered there was a young Kampa woman who had died. Many lamas carried her body up to an altar to present her to the white eagles. There was nothing on her body. Only the eagles feeding on it. I was overwhelmed by a deep sense of solemnity. This feeling still overwhelms me today. It makes you realize that there are many beautiful things relating to life. Therefore, I think Shangri-La is a palace in another realm, where the spirit of the white eagles, where the vast nature and all lives come together peacefully in Shangri-La."

"In the Tibetan sky funeral, a person's body completely returns to nature, right?"

"A sky funeral is the funeral style that we Tibetans recognize as the best, because when you are dead, it is best to contribute your flesh to the white eagles and let them transport you to another place. Just letting your flesh rot is not as good as letting the white eagles feed on it and transport it to another realm in the sky. I believe it is a beautiful and the most natural experience. I believe that Shangri-La is related to this concept."

"What do you feel when you paint the white eagles?"

"I feel like I am the white eagle's spirit. Sometimes, I feel like my parents, who are simple people. The white eagle and our family have no great differences between us. You see, my father is quite pure as well."

Ang Sang went on to explain his other art. He pointed to the painting of Guan Yin, with the face of his cousin, Yang Jin. "The thousand-hand-thousand-eye Guan Yin has many hands to help many people who are in difficulty. She has many eyes to see all those who are in need. This is close to my own beliefs. So I paint these hands and eyes as they have a feeling of order. This is to allow more people to understand and know that there are many people who still live in poverty, who do not have enough to eat or wear and need others' help. If more people can help one another with pure action, they in turn will be repaid for their compassion. A person must study how to really be a person. To really be a person is to be pure. Religion is one form of purity. Through this; through interaction with all kinds of people and through your own words, you can let others know you, as I have let them know me through my paintings. Through the third eye of Buddha, one can see all the things that man can see, understand others and understand oneself. Then one will become relaxed, and one's realization will come naturally. People's hearts are expressed through their eyes. Regardless of our expressions, our eyes can express the most. In my heart, the Shangri-La I search for can be sought through the

third eye of Buddha."

Tibetan Kampa women are another favorite theme of Ang Sang's paintings. "I see that you paint many Kampa women, who exude a feeling of beauty and power. Can you explain this feeling to me?"

"I like to paint the women of many Tibetan regions. They give one a feeling of tremendous power and greatness. If you go to the northern Tibetan grasslands, you can see them standing in the freezing cold with many children running about the grasslands without adequate clothing. These are children of the grasslands and their lifestyle is actually quite wonderful. The love of their mothers has given me a deep impression. In that harsh and terrible landscape, they can raise children to become adults — these women have greatness. I want to express the greatness of Kampa mothers in my paintings. They have a Buddha in their hearts and live in the land of spirits. Their eyes are beautiful like the eyes of a Buddha. In many of my paintings, I also depict the unique clothing and jewelry of Tibetan women."

"I see that you put power into the hands and eyes of the women that you paint. Can you tell me the background of the clothing you depict in your paintings?"

"From the time I left university, I designed stage sets and costumes for dance troupes. Tibetan clothing is special and very colorful, which is different from that of other ethnic groups. In one small county, you can discover many different styles of clothing. You can feel their hearts from their clothing. For instance, Tibetan women like to wear very thick necklaces that are made of stones and turquoise. Their aprons will have many contrasting colors like a rainbow. Their hairstyles, which are adorned with precious stones, are beautiful. I want to express many beautiful things in what I paint and present them to everyone, especially the Kampa women. Whatever they own, whatever they have, they wear them on their bodies. Once, I went to Chengdu for the annual regional art show, and the Kampa women there dressed beautifully. They wore so much jewelry on their bodies that they could hardly walk. Several of these women had to be carried onto the stage. Some wore over ten million *renminbi* worth of jewels on their bodies. They expressed a profound feeling of the Tibetans by taking the most beautiful things and bringing them to others. Tibetan turquoise and corals go best with their clothing and fit beautifully as jewelry. Therefore, they love the "nine-eye" stones, which can protect them from evil. Tibetans live in a harsh and terrible environment, and therefore, they must protect themselves from the elements. So in my paintings, I express the power that the jewelry possesses."

"Is Shangri-La in Tibet?"

"It is said that Tibet is the last place where the environment has not been destroyed, and it is where people who love the environment want to protect it. Artists should let the world understand the importance of nature and the environment, of history and of eternal culture. Each person must be responsible in protecting these things. My inspiration comes from here. I have gone to many places like Beijing, but I cannot leave this place, which is my source. Here, I can find the best things inside my heart. Here, there is a wonderful religion and a well-protected environment. I hope that these things can be kept alive forever. Man and nature should be in harmony forever."

"But you haven't answered my question. Where is Shangri-La?"

"It is a beautiful thing, an ideal that is in your mind. Every person has a Shangri-La in their hearts and minds. In mine, I have a Buddha, and this is my painting. It is also my lifestyle, which I love. This is my Shangri-La. Wherever you go to look for Shangri-La is irrelevant. The most important is your heart because if you have this inside your heart, you can find Shangri-La wherever you go."

Ang Sang then spread on his bed designs of different Tibetan clothes that he was working on. Some designs were finished; others still being drawn. These designs were to be used by the Tibetan dance troupes as costumes, which were being manufactured at a factory by disabled Tibetans. The factory only produced Tibetan crafts, clothing, medicinal incense, papers, and other crafts. Ang Sang offered to take me to the factory for a visit if I wanted to. So we went.

There were fifty handicapped Tibetans working in the factory called the Lhasa Handicapped Handicraft Center. They relied their livelihood on the factory. It was also their home, their social circle, their lives. Jampa Tsundhup, the factory director, gave them a direction in life, as well as opportunities and hope. When two disabled workers got married, he represented their families as their paternal father. In many cases, the disabled workers did not have any other family members to attend their wedding.

He had started the factory with little money, with neither outside support nor funding from the government. In the beginning, they had to cook on open fires in the cold of the night as there was no kitchen. Jampa Tsundhup, the factory director, was once a lama. He discarded his robes and left the monastery to bring his belief to those who needed it most. He was a Bodhisattva.

In addition to supporting themselves, the fifty disabled workers also supported one hundred Tibetan orphans, many of whom were also disabled. Jampa Tsundhup was also the headmaster of Lhasa Jatson Chumig Welfare Special School for the orphans, which he had built on the small compound with the proceeds from the factory. They lived in the school and attended classes in Chinese and Tibetan languages. They also sang songs that they wrote. I called San Bao on my mobile and asked him to come over to the school to listen to their songs. He came immediately. The children were thrilled to see a star like San Bao. They surrounded him.

They sang:

"To see a grand eagle, soaring in the sky, you do not know where he is flying.

"Coming to this school, we realize the value of life, wild flowers are blooming...

"On the first day entering school, half belief half doubt, like a dream...

"We are grateful for this opportunity in life, it is too sad not to know your own culture...

"To realize beautiful dreams, please do not pass the good years in vain."

Their song captured the stillness of the late Tibetan afternoon, when sunlight was the strongest and the shadows became deep, protruding abstractions of one's imagination. The sorrow of their condition was drowned in the joy of their singing. They were overcoming predicament.

Finding Directions

I dialed one of the numbers which Douglas Gerber gave me the day I arrived in Lhasa. I spoke to a Tibetan who knew that the Living Buddha, His Eminence Beru Khyentse Rimpoche, would be arriving in Lhasa any day. But he was not sure which day or where he would stay. He suggested that I call one of the other numbers Douglas gave me. Which one? Any one, it did not matter. Just call. If Rimpoche arrives, he will see you.

So I called. I sat on the top floor of a Nepalese café overlooking the square of Jokhang Temple, eating Tibetan *momo* dumplings with *zamba* wheat flour crushed into barley sticks, drinking yak butter tea. When it proved that all of the telephone numbers could not offer me a clue to when Rimpoche would arrive or where he would stay, I began to look for him in my cup of yak butter tea. I could not find him. Maybe I was not looking carefully enough. Then one of his friends arrived in the square looking for me. After several telephone calls, we made contact. Yes, Rimpoche had arrived. He had arrived the previous night but had not told anybody. This was the way Rimpoche preferred to arrive and leave. This would give him adequate time away from all of those who wanted to follow him, so that he could go alone to Jokhang Temple, light incense and feel the energy projected by hundreds of Tibetan prayer wheels turning. So if we wanted to find Rimpoche, we should go to Jokhang Temple and look around.

We should try to feel the energy there and if it is flowing in the right direction, then maybe we can find Rimpoche.

This would require staying at Jokhang Temple, hanging out with the monks and feeling the energy in the temple. It would require turning off the mobile phone, not making any more calls and listening to the chanting of the monks without interruption, simply imagine that. It seemed so simple, yet so difficult. I had to imagine, so I stared at the steam rising from a cup of yak butter tea and smelled the yak butter. I prepared myself to turn off the mobile phone. Upon pressing the "off" button, my mind was transported to a prairie field stretching into the horizon, as far as one could stretch the limits of his imagination. At the tip of my imagination, I could see wild Tibetan ponies running in uncertain directions. I thought about the ponies and wondered what they were looking for. They were running. The direction was uncertain. They just kept running.

This was the point at which I threw my mobile phone into a trash can that was strategically placed near the Jokhang Temple plaza by the Lhasa Municipal Health Department, for the purpose of receiving unwanted scraps of paper, used Kodak film boxes, cigarette butts, and disinherited mobile phones. I went to Jokhang Temple to listen to the monks, as well as to find Rimpoche. It was fortunate that I turned off my mobile phone before throwing it into the trash can, otherwise its ringing might upset people who walked past the trash can. They might have traveled long distances and searching for something they could not find because their direction

was uncertain.

We could not find Rimpoche. We waited at Jokhang Temple and listened to the monks chanting. We waited. We looked. But we could not find Rimpoche. Suddenly, it occurred to me that he might try to call me on my mobile phone, which I had just dropped into the trash can. So we went back into Jokhang Temple plaza to retrieve it. It was still in the trash can where I had left it because it did not ring, and nobody was disturbed by its presence because I had turned it off.

As I wiped the dust off the mobile phone, my friend noticed somebody calling us from atop a building in the plaza. He was standing on the balcony of a Tibetan restaurant. The man wore the yellow robes of a senior monk. He was waving. It was Rimpoche's assistant. Instead of finding him, he had found us. I became acutely aware of the fact that we were being found by the person whom we were looking for in the complete absence of electronic digitized communication. I suddenly realized that the first step toward finding Shangri-La would be the conscious act of throwing away one's mobile telephone. It would be in the process of recovering something that had been discarded, which we felt is essential, but in fact, was not. I finally realized how important it is to dispossess oneself of the things that we find so convenient.

Rimpoche smiled as I made my way upstairs to the restaurant balcony. He hardly said anything but indicated that he had found me. In fact, he had not moved from his seat, eating a bowl of yellow rice the whole time. He had become aware of my frantic

search to find him and had asked his assistant to wave to us as we looked for a discarded mobile phone. Yes, he had gone to Jokhang Temple when we were there and had left without us knowing. We were looking too hard. Therefore, we could not find what we were looking for. So he found us instead.

Rimpoche was born in Lhasa. He started studying Buddhism at the age of seven. Now, he travels the world lecturing and teaching meditation. "I always talk to people in public, at universities, and every place I go. I talk of compassion, how to make peace with the self and with others, as well as with the environment. People are very interested," he nodded.

"How have you been?" he asked. I told him that I had decided to quit being a lawyer, an economist and a business advisor to foreign multinational corporations coming to China. I was no longer going to help anyone make money, and I was not going to make any myself. At forty-one, I had decided to discard the career I had so painfully and carefully built up. I would throw it out like the mobile phone, which had been turned off. I was now going through the painful process of disconnecting.

"What are you going to do?" he asked. I told him I was going to produce films about Shangri-La. He thought that it was a good idea and worth pursuing as more people would need to start searching for Shangri-La. The problem would be to find out exactly where Shangri-La was. This process would require more disconnecting. This would be the difficult part. It would require separation of the immaterial from the material, placing the pieces in front of you, and understanding which ones to be discarded and which ones to retain. Such a process would require reducing everything to the bare essential.

"Materialism will temporarily make you happy," Rimpoche explained. "Money and wealth seem to give people a sense of peace, but usually they cause more suffering. If you have more material things, more possessions, more to take care of, more to desire, you have more suffering. We call it desire. People always look for more because they are not satisfied. Buddhism teaches that you should be contented with just enough money and enough possessions, instead of pursuing more. Then you will be happy, otherwise, you will never be satisfied. Because most people have a material life, they are very busy keeping up with the material. They become stressed up and very unhappy. So they ask me how to release the stress through learning Buddhist philosophy and meditation."

Rimpoche never speaks about Buddhism as a religion. He refers to it as a philosophy. He teaches meditation, not religion. Teaching is a process of learning. "When you learn more, you want to know more," he explained to me. "It is very, very profound. Other religions are also very great, but Buddhism always gives the chance for one to know the answer. Not that you should believe. When you feel it is right, you can start practicing Buddhism. If you do not feel so, there is no need to follow Buddhism. Buddhism offers one choices. Buddha said his teaching is like gold. When you buy gold, you should put it into fire and test it. If it is beneficial to you, then practice it. If not, just leave it. Most other religions say you have to follow, you have no choice. Buddhism will let your decision be dependent on your own wish. So when I travel, many people ask questions. I gave them the answers, and most people are happy with my answers."

So I took the opportunity to ask a question. "Where is Shangri-La?"

"The search for Shangri-La is not new," Rimpoche explained. "Many had tried to follow this road before, and most got lost. In the years between 1962 up until around 1973, many people in Europe and America sought happiness in drugs, but most of them were not happy. Some people even died taking drugs. I had helped people quit drugs, to make peace with themselves. At that time, most people were drug addicts. Now, it is not the same. People of all ages are seeking inner peace and happiness. They started doing social work to help the less fortunate, in Tibet and Qinghai, many people have problems — sickness, absence of education, shortage of medicine — they suffer greatly. So I give them education. I started a school and this year, a clinic. There are monks and nuns who want to practice and I give them the opportunity. In social work, I helped them built three bridges. I help poor people, many of whom are old, and young children without education. I am happy to do this, apart from religion itself, as it brings happiness to people. I hope in the future, I can do more to help people. Yes, it requires much effort."

I told him I was on my way to Qinghai. "Traveling is

dangerous," he explained with a word of caution. "Much more dangerous in Qinghai. One must travel many days by car. One day, I had an accident and my car went off the road. I did not die but the car was damaged," he shrugged, matter-of-factly. "Lhasa is my home," explained Rimpoche. "Every time I traveled, I came back here. I remembered I was here when I was six years old. I came here to join 200 lamas in chanting."

The chanting of 200 lamas overwhelmed my mind like a rush of waves over rocks. Then the sound of lamas vanished and I felt silence — the sound of one's mind going blank but becoming clear against the pulse of the heart beating through one's mind like a fat red drum.

Rimpoche could see this at the back of my mind, as if he was looking at a mirror from behind its reflection against the light of another mirror, from which a candle burned with the anticipation of the wax melting shortly but not as quickly as one might expect. "Lhasa is still the center of Tibet and Shangri-La," he interrupted my thought. The fat red drum stopped beating, for just a moment. So if Lhasa is Shangri-La, then the search for Shangri-La could end where it had begun?

Rimpoche explained that according to Tibetan philosophy, we are now in the age of Kali, a time of seemingly endless war, pestilence and suffering. This period would one day be followed by the future. "Shambhala is Shangri-La," Rimpoche explained. "Shambhala is the future king. There will be suffering and peace. There are four continents — south, east, west, and north — where

Shangri-La is. It exists but you cannot get there. In this world, we have many disasters and wars. In Shangri-La, we all look for something else — a future continent — a time of peace. I think they are looking for the future. Some call it Shambhala, others call it Shangri-La, which is a very popular term. The world is now smaller because of modern communication. But Shangri-La cannot be reached through telecommunication. If you practice meditation, you can reach Shangri-La." That was all he said. He stood up slowly and left. The monks in attendance, silent throughout our conversation, followed behind him. As the saffron robes brushed past, Rimpoche left as he arrived, unexpected.

Departure

The main street around Jokhang Temple is shaped like a Chinese hexagram. So if one flew above Jokhang Temple and looked down, one would find a great Chinese hexagram with the temple in the center like a *ba-gua* (Eight Trigram). Energy emanates from the temple. It circles like the many people in the street outside, turning the prayer wheels. The wheels turn and with them, a concentric energy which seems to draw endless numbers of Tibetans on their pilgrimages to the temple.

Behind Jokhang Temple, there is an Internet bar. It is called the Yellow Room. Actually, it was a secret tea room of the 6th Dalai Lama (1683-1706). He used to come to the Yellow Room to write poetry in tranquility. Now, the Yellow Room is an Internet bar. Young travelers come here to drink chai masala, an Indian milk tea, eat banana pancakes and get online.

A girl with purple hair and silver Tibetan bracelets running up both arms came down the stairway from a rooftop garden of the Yellow Room. She had been sitting in the afternoon shadows looking for Shangri-La in a cup of chai masala. She switched on a computer and began to surf the Internet. I asked her where she was from and whether she could help me send an e-mail to a friend.

"You're from Guangzhou?"

"Yes, I am from Guangzhou."

"How long have you been here?"

"Hmm. I think two weeks. No, it's already sixteen days."

"Sixteen days? Why did you leave Guangzhou, where you have everything you want, and come to Lhasa?"

"How should I answer that? I am studying film-making, so I thought Lhasa is a good place to make a film. One day, maybe, I will make such a film. This is only one of the reasons. Another reason is because Lhasa is mysterious, exuding religious colors. I came with what I believed packed in my baggage. Maybe I will leave without my baggage. Maybe I am a Buddhist in disguise."

"Guangzhou is such a developed, modern city — a materialist place. I can't understand why you came here."

"Guangzhou is too noisy and crass. Life there is too fast and competition is fierce. People there have become noisy and crass."

"So you came here looking for something?"

"Yes, I came looking for the Tibetan spirit."

"I see that you collect Tibetan jewelry."

"I like these kinds of artsy things."

"This is chic, new fashion."

"This is new fashion? I don't reckon so. It's just what I like. I like to collect Tibetan things. By the way, getting on the Internet here is slow. It may still take a while. What do you want to write in this e-mail."

"Write to aijing@aijing.com. Just say: 'I am in Lhasa, but I still cannot find 'Shangri-La' .'"

"That's it?"

"That's it."

"Ok. I understand. By the way, I don't think you can find Shangri-La in Lhasa."

"Why?"

"Because the Lhasa my friends told me about is already not like what they had told me. It is not the way it should be. It is too commercialized. You have to go to Namutsuo Lake. It is a more difficult place to get to than here. There, at Namutsuo, you will feel the real profoundness. You may find what you are looking for."

"So if one wants to find Shangri-La, one should leave Lhasa and travel to Namutsuo Lake. Is that what you're saying? "

"Namutsuo is a really beautiful, a good place to shoot a film."

"Really? Then are you saying that I should go to Namutsuo Lake?"

"Yeah, but not necessarily. This depends on whether the lake is calling you. If it calls, then go."

I went. On the way, I found a pile of stones. What moves a stone? Wind, rain, sand, or a bigger stone?

The Tibetans pray to nature. A *manidui* is made up of stones piled one on top of another, covered with *jingfan* prayer flags. These stone piles will be placed upon different centers of energy. *Jingfan* prayer flags may be draped across a road, an important shrine, or a point of departure.

Sometimes, a yak's skull is placed upon the *manidui*, usually with special care and attention, without moving a single stone. The yak's skull might have been picked clean by white eagles and its bone whitened by the wind and sun.

A *manidui* is a good place to visit alone, to sit and watch a stone and ask oneself how long the stone has been left untouched. Is the placing of stones upon a *manidui* part of a design or a plan? Were the stones intentionally placed here, to be found by someone else? Whose hands placed the stones? Were the hands that placed the stones carved of wind, dust and stone as well? In the relationship between a hand and a stone, the space for margin of error is impossible. Its intention deliberate.

You may try to have a conversation with the yak's skull. Dialogue may be difficult. He will laugh at you and the white eagles will fly away in distress. At this point, you will become acutely aware that there is no heaven above, no hell below. There is nothing behind and nothing in front. At this point, the indicators are pointing in parallel directions. By thinking you had reached the end of the road, it is only a point of departure from the beginning of where you have been. Now your senses can be clear. There is only one direction — ahead.

Behind the *manidui*, there is a range of snow-capped mountains, lost in mist, and sometimes, rain. Above the rain, there is snow. The Tibetans say that amidst the snows at a point that is roughly 5,000 meters above sea level, there is a palace of snows, which cannot be found because the place is too cold and far away. The palace is the home of Nianjia Tangle, the protector of nomads, sheep and yaks. The protector spirit lives in the palace of snows. He rides a stunningly beautiful white horse. The mane is fine, like snow.

On the road to Namutsuo Lake, one is reminded to stop at a *manidui* wrapped in white *hada* scarves and colorful *jingfan*. Finding the *manidui* is not difficult. One must look for a place before the snow-capped mountains, where energy is emitted from the skull of a yak, which still has mats of black yak hair attached to flesh that the white eagles have forgotten to strip clean or was left behind for some unexplained reason. If one needs to know a reason, ask the white eagles. High monks at sky funeral altars call them by their names. So can you.

One knows that this is the correct *manidui* because upon reaching this place, you will feel a sense of departure. Remember this: look ahead to the road that leads to a dirt road, which eventually leads to no road at all, but that will eventually lead you to Namutsuo Lake. Follow the road until it ceases to exist and you will have arrived at the lake. As you travel this road before it ceases to be a road, you will become acutely aware of the dimensions of space and time around you that you were always convinced you understood, but now you do not. Do not look back at the yak's skull because it will confuse you. It may not be where you thought it was when you left. Only the white eagles can be sure and precise about this question.

As you travel the road, you will feel the earth touches heaven at a point where the horizon becomes apparent. And you will realize when you have reached the horizon that the heaven touches earth. This will occur when you reach the edge of Namutsuo Lake, a place of distinct departure. Because at Namutsuo Lake, before

the vastness of a salt-water lake, which appears to be the sea, realization occurs that you cannot go any further.

Before snow-capped mountains, pray for protection from the spirit on a white horse. Rain will arrive. It will cover the mountains from your view, and then, it too, will disappear. If you see a rainbow, you may mistake it for a spirit on a white horse. He has already come and gone too. If you hear thunder, listen without fear. It is only a resounding voice of protection. The echo is your own thoughts standing on the Tibetan plateau grassland, full of flowers in the rain, clapping your hands alone. If you do not pay attention, the rainbow will soon be gone too. So do not stop looking for the spirit on a white horse. He will eventually arrive. Just wait. Close your eyes. Remember, do not let the altitude disorient you. Confusion is unnecessary. This means that you cannot stay here very long but should leave a prayer with a white *hada* scarf tied to a rock to this place. You must then leave immediately. Do not look back.

Searching for Soundless Sound

You explained to me the most important element of sound is no sound.
To find this you must close the door and close your eyes.
Can sound filter in?
Can you escape the sounds which juxtapose sound?

Climb 4,000 meters above sea.
Listen to wind and sky.
The passing of clouds is soundless.
But the cry of eagles is not.
A lone white eagle's last cry
becomes sound without sound.

A yak's bell, a lama's horn
the chanting of a nomad
alone in a valley
with sheep and yak,
alone with only the sound
of oneself chanting.
When chanting is over,
the sound of one's voice fades
into wind of another valley
remembered only by an echo
of clouds passing.

Qinghai

Connecting with a Stone

After leaving Tibet, I traveled to Qinghai. The road was long and I often slept on the back seat of trucks or jeeps that I was lucky enough to flag down. Drivers were not used to stopping for hitchhikers, especially a foreign one. But some stopped, partly out of interest, partly for amusement. One old driver kept practicing his English with me the whole time, the whole long road. I could not sleep. I could not think. I could not look out the window at what was passing by. He just kept speaking English to me. Finally, I got off and just walked.

The summer sky was pristine blue, an occasional white cloud passed overhead. The road stretched across rock, mountain platitudes of grassland, expanses of one's mind unfolding like waves churning in a vast sea of space which has not been limited by design or structure. I followed this process of deconstruction. The road led somewhere, but it was in the inconclusiveness of not being sure where that somewhere would lead to that the road became worth following. So I followed.

I must have been hitchhiking and was probably dumped off a jeep or a truck when I came upon a tea shop, the kind which sells nothing much except tea and yak butter tea. I ordered a cup of yak butter tea when a girl walked in and sat behind me. She was covered with Tibetan turquoise, but I knew right away that she was not Tibetan. She wore a bandanna around her head and huge earrings. I knew from her composure that she was not a nomad. Was she a gypsy in disguise?

She was the fashion designer, Flora Cheong-leen, known throughout China as Zhang Tianai. A friend I had known from my years in Hong Kong and Beijing, I did not expect to find her here, collecting turquoise and Tibetan weavings. She too was traveling throughout western China, searching for elements to inspire new fashion designs in the elements of Shangri-La.

Flora Cheong-leen — fashion diva, famous designer, brand, label — an image in high-end shopping malls covered with white marble, the kind you can see your reflection in when there are not too many people walking or where you can slide across when wearing Bally shoes after the janitor in white-starched janitor shirt has mopped the white marble. I stared at my reflection in the white yak butter and pretended it was the fancy marble floor of one of those shopping malls, covered in quick drying cement along the old crippled ancient alleyways of Beijing. I liked to wander through them on an autumn day when the leaves had already turned gold, yet not dry enough to fall and be carried away, dreamlike, by the wind.

It was a rainy late summer day, the kind one wants to be sitting in a Tibetan tea house, drinking yak butter tea. Just one of those yak butter tea days, the kind which leaves one sitting at an old wooden table, looking out the window, counting raindrops.

I counted. Flora counted too. When we ran out of raindrops, we began to talk.

After staring at my slowly expanding raindrop in a flat surface of yak butter tea which one could pretend was a high-end shopping mall, I finally asked Flora why Tibetan chic was now becoming chic everywhere else, except in Tibet. "People are looking for what is the next in fashion," she explained. "Fashion started from Paris. The French wanted to look like Italians and the Italians like the Americans and the Americans like the British; we then had the prep look. It is all hollow, no substance. You don't dress like a nun because you believe in Catholicism. Everything depends on economy and politics. Look at the politics. Can you trust anything? Enron, accountants, war on the horizon... Look at China, a five-thousand-year history, and Tibet — its history gives people a secure feeling because it has lasted so long. So what if China has gone up and down, and up and down? The fact that it has lasted so long makes people feel good to just know that."

"Then what you're really saying is this new ethnic Shangri-La style is not a fad but a reaction against the globalization movement of the 1990s, which many associate with ultra-materialist values?" I took a sip of hot yak butter tea and tried to swallow what I had just said.

"It is not just a reaction because I think people today are really lost. People are saying, 'Hey look, I am swimming around in all of this materialism. I have black pants, blue pants, white pants and all of these things and look like a robot.' This robot-like outfit system gives me no security. At the same time, Western material values are messing with a lot of global people, threatening their ethnicity — the things which give one identity and a sense of security. People don't understand what's really happening, so they react through their dressing. The combination of colors and beads and the mixture of the old and new are things which make them feel fulfilled. This is evidence that some things lasted so long and are still continuing."

"But in many ways, it seems that Chinese ethnic chic is being re-imported back into China after becoming accepted as vogue in Paris and Milan," I pressed for Flora's views.

"Milan and Paris are where they set the standards. Asia follows the West. China has just opened up only over the past few years, so they think what they have is no good. It is nothing," Flora picked up a piece of traditional ethnic brocade she had been thumbing on the table and held it forward for me to touch. "This has been going on for ages and ages in the streets of China. Crochet for table cloth or anything. All these big magazines and American media are just putting it into the current mainstream. Promotion is making it come back from the darkness of forgotten traditions. Media has all the control and they can import anything. The Chinese have always had it, but it does not have any special value to them because it does not have a brand name on it. So they create a brand look-a-like. They need that identity."

Flora then took a sip of yak butter tea and thought about what she had just said. Fingering a string of Tibetan corals which I knew she was imagining could be repackaged with a touch of something else and turned into a Fifth Avenue fashion item with a price tag to reflect the rent. "About the West using our ethnic traditional things," she went on staring into her cup, "I think it is very simple; they have run out of their own stuff. Pop and fast-food lifestyle packaged in a can is just not enough. It lacks emotion and moreover, most of the people have not traveled out of their own realm, so they do not know anything else. Look, 80% of Americans don't even have a passport! So when you present these people with Asian ethnic, they are shocked and at the same time stimulated by it. Even people from other parts of Asia, say Singapore, have not been to these places and are stimulated by it too. Meanwhile, the media promotes it. The West promotes it. Armani and Gucci are now using ethnic things because they are somebody. So they think it is a Western thing." Then she looked into her cup of yak butter tea, very carefully.

"Where does tea come from? How is water transcended into our cup? We people come from somewhere. This is our soul. Designing is thinking. Things come from here. The West is coming up with ethnic designs so suddenly and ethnic fashion comes from there. But if you go back a long time, all these ethnic things come from China."

"Then Chinese or ethnic Shangri-La chic is a fusion of East-meets-West style plus values. Or am I missing something?"

"Many Asian and Western designers make use of the actual product, say antique patches. They go and look for some ethnic-driven handicrafts and merge them to the clothes. Such a style is popular. A number of designers in Europe and America are putting folklore craft into their works. I am different. People like comfort. Maybe, because I am Chinese, a dancer, as well as a sportswoman, I design what suits my lifestyle best. The design of my pants is big bell-bottom hipster because the future is driven by natural sexuality. I add patches of Chinese ethnic fabrics and Tibetan leather to give them impact. Life is nothing but clashes and how you render them. There is no East meets West. I am very

Westernized, yet very Chinese and very futuristic. My state of mind and life is like a snow mountain, and to me, future is about fusion. If you do not fuse, there is no future. If you are single-mindedly isolated in the bottom of a well, you are isolated. If not, you must fuse in culture and people. Remember, there are no boundaries."

"Then for you, Flora, returning to China, traveling to these isolated areas, is in a way a search for your own ethnicity. Yeah?"

"When I did costumes at the Royal Ballet, I realized that the future is only what people tell you it is. You go to a design school and when you graduate, people tell you you're a great designer. Why? They tell you sleeves are supposed to look like this and there are so many sleeves. No, they come from somewhere. Everything comes from somewhere. Food comes from somewhere. A buffet comes from somewhere. Fusion food, sushi and noodles all come from somewhere. Nobody ever asks. People are born in a place. So I began exploring my roots, which brought me back to China. I had forgotten, living in the West, that I was Chinese. Now I am back in China. I have no choice. All things have a connection with how the ethnic groups called for rain and life; the hope in the search for heaven. That is where movements start from the energy connecting from the diaphragm, my energy transcends to you, to everyone."

"Then people are searching for something else, something beyond. They are just disillusioned. Right?" I looked into my cup of yak butter tea, searching for disillusionment.

"People need much more space for illusion and hope. Western people's life is a repeat of everything, the same street corner, same fashion shop. Western culture has created a world of material repetition. People live with stereotypes. So everyone is coming here in search of something, instead of just tangible materialism. This is an era of change. Asians have it, but they cannot see it. They have thousands of years of thinking but they do not want to see it. They only keep building concrete jungles. All they see are the repeated brand names and their desire to look like everybody else. They are in fact lost."

"Then yours is a rejection of the material, a realization that materialism can only bring you this far? But haven't you been accused by Hong Kong paparazzi of being a material girl?"

"I can shamefully say I have everything under the sun, from houses, cars, friends, power, money, to fame. It's shameful because when I go home, I realize they are all superficial. All this materialism is not constructive." Showing me a Tibetan necklace she had collected, Flora pointed to the crude uncut raw turquoise stones with her fine fingernail. "This is not a diamond, but these are real stones. Since I have been meditating, traveling around China and visiting beautiful mountains, this is what gives me security because this has an energy that is a form of power from the earth. Vibrant energy gives me security because I feel connected, and it brings me a sense of balance. It has nothing to do with city values. So what if I have a diamond ring that is worth thousands of dollars and wear it on the street so that everyone can look at me and say, 'Wow, she's rich!' So what? It just makes me feel cheap. I feel raped. My values have now changed."

Flora then carefully laid all the Tibetan turquoise rings and other things she had been collecting on the rough wooden table for me to look at. We looked at each piece, which emanates with the energy of the mountains from which it came. "Look at these people," Flora pointed out of the window at the Tibetans passing in the rain, their faces covered with colorful bandannas, "They have been riding horses on the plains, eating natural food, that is how life should be and that is how God made us. We've been putting ourselves into a dark hole that is like a prison, where we have to manufacture everything. Sometimes, we manufacture and design so much of our lives that we are just ruining everything in the end. For some, searching for Shangri-La is a reaction to the cycle, for others, they do not know where they are going, so they are hoping to connect with something through the process of searching."

"Then how does one connect to a stone?" I asked.

"Natural stone is becoming an important part of everyone's life, whether in chandeliers, jewelry, or furniture. Stone is metaphysical, spiritual, and physical. Stones make you feel good because their colors embody all the elements. And when you are alone, you feel the energy connecting into you through their visual beauty. It is a philosophy you believe in. The stone has energy. So we realize that we must connect ourselves, otherwise we will not be able to connect to a piece of stone. I would rather be seen in this," she picked up a Tibetan silver ring inlaid with chunks of rough turquoise and coral, "than some million-dollar diamond which is nothing other than a brand name. Diamonds are forever. I do not want to belong to that philosophy anymore nor live this life of brands and money. My values have changed. "

"You built an entire fashion brand 'Tian Art' around the concept of integrating China's traditional 'five elements' and juxtaposing their colors. Why have you embraced the five elements as part of your own philosophy?"

"The five elements in my designs have all the colors of the five elements of the Chinese tradition: gold, fire, earth, water and wood. I want to design clothes for people who will feel the elements themselves internally, which help them feel the emotional balance, without which you too will be in a state of turmoil all the time. Remember, the elements are first physical, then emotional, last spiritual. Without that extra energy, you cannot live modern life. So you have to get that spirituality, ran to Tibet first, get spiritual, then the physical and emotional will follow. Remember, don't get mental. All this mental state fixes people in a hierarchy where they are condemning and judgmental, becoming unnecessarily political. Then it upsets everything."

"Then it is the spiritual which you are seeking here?"

"The most important is spiritual belief because ultimately I will leave the earth when I get old. Imagine saying to one's kid, 'Darling, mommy is dying but you must have a big house. If I leave you with this big house, you have to do things in this big house. If I leave you with a million dollars, you have to spend it.' Do you think life will be easy for them? Life is how you live it. This material lifestyle is now a religion and money is a fixation that is actually harming everyone without them knowing it. Ruthlessly, without boundaries or edge, people's attitude is 'for money, I will do anything'. So now I travel to mountains, rivers in the western part of China and go north. It's all about different emotions, feelings and cultures which really enforces our natural goodness, rather than the manufactured things."

"So Flora, tell me, what are you really doing here?" I took another sip of yak butter tea and felt its warmth circulate within against the cool late summer rain beating on the edge of window. "Don't tell me you are also searching for Shangri-La."

"I come here for Zen — a peace of mind. It is a power of feelings and peace over one's mind. A natural connection to the land makes me feel its power. Having a natural connection with heaven, water, woods and trees, I feel I am in heaven because I am the happiest that way. When I first saw the movie about Shangri-La — *Lost Horizon* — I think heaven is like that. I was brought up believing in heaven and hell. But that's lateral. Searching for Shangri-La goes beyond searching for Shangri-La. This is because Shangri-La is a place beyond a place, beyond the horizon. When you close your eyes, you can think about it any way and that is Shangri-La. It is the security of your energy, soul and balance, without any dependence on anyone — your boss, your husband, your lover, your clothing, your material satisfaction. I can have a glass of water and a bowl of rice and be happy. That is my Shangri-La."

"What about the search for Shangri-La?"

"To me, the search for Shangri-La is all about the intention in my mind. I am referring to positive intention. I live a fusion lifestyle. There are no clashes for me between regions, cultures and people. This comes together with a connection of the past and the present, through traveling and experiencing everything. If you do not experience, you cannot fuse because you will be stuck with limited vocabulary. People and culture must fuse, only then you can find Shangri-La. You must search without searching, but you cannot search without knowledge. Maybe for some people, if they are gifted, they can search for it while they are looking in Tibet and Yunnan. But sometimes, it just comes only before you die, or maybe with lightning and thunder, or maybe back in your office in the most materialistic period of your life. It could be like a fever you overcome and then wake up to it. It can be caused by anything. But the most important is connection."

"Am I taking the right road to Shangri-La?"

"Connection is a point. Tibet is a point. But to say I have been there and now I am holistic is just hearsay. Everyone has his own story and journey. You will find many, many people at different levels. It all depends on who you meet. There are thousands of levels of connection, don't ever forget this. Remember, it is a long, long road you are about to take, and it is at that level that you must connect."

Flora then looked out the window. The raindrops kept falling. Tibetan nomads were still passing outside with their faces wrapped in colorful bandannas and chunks of raw turquoise sewn into their hair. Only black forlorn eyes peered from behind the bandannas wrapped across their faces. Flora nodded toward the nomads, or gypsies.

"The gypsies are connected with heaven and earth. They can live anywhere. They have no fixed form of lifestyle. They keep themselves warm and comfortable and are happy with each other. It is a life without a pre-set image of their aims. They go with the flow of nature. They live in harmony with the five Chinese elements of water, wood, fire, earth and gold. It is such a struggle for us to go back to nature because we are all manufactured. But gypsies, they have already found Shangri-La. The Tibetans call it Shambhala, meaning, the future. If you look for the future, you will doubt it, unless you go back to something. Nothing comes from and goes to nothing. So you live this life for nothing."

I realized my first guess might just be right. Maybe Flora was a gypsy in disguise.

Nothing Left

Qinghai. I was searching for nomads. They are hard to find. Being nomads, they are constantly on the move, changing their location. They move like wind. You cannot keep up. When you try to find them, they disperse. Locating them is difficult because you must concentrate on their act of dispersion.

To find nomads, you must follow a road that leads you to no particular direction and you have to keep following it. The problem is that nomads keep a distance from the roads. They travel where there are no roads. This is what differentiates them from us. It is what makes them nomads.

To find the exact location of the nomads will require a "tool", not a compass or a map. This involves a ball of string. It is quite difficult for most people to imagine how a ball of string will help. But it is actually quite simple. To find nomads requires unraveling a ball of string.

A ball of string is formed by wrapping around itself from different directions until it becomes a tight ball without a discernible end. It provides no space for flexibility and is a complete solid mass which, in fact, has no solid foundation. It is only because it has been interwoven over itself, logically and systematically wrapped twisted upon its own internal emptiness that the string can exist in its own self-paralyzing state. This is the state of twisted string.

A mind can be like a ball of twisted string. So can a human body. Hold a ball of twisted string aloft in the air and pretend that a kite has been attached to the string and this kite is an eagle, carried into the air in concentric waves under its wings. The ball of string will unravel. There will be a momentary feeling of anticipation that all which has been so carefully wrapped will soon be undone, that careful and logical process of creating a tight ball of string may be undone. This idea can threaten one's instincts and put them off guard. In the process of unraveling comes the freedom of unwrapping something which deserves to be freed. In fact, it is meant to be undone.

From this point, you can begin to understand the rationale of following a road into Qinghai which leads to nowhere. Qinghai means "green sea" in Chinese. It is a green sea in all four directions. The land is green. There are green hills and mountains, green rivers and lakes, green reflected in a blue sky. Stand in the green and look up at the blue sky and twist your body in concentric circles but do not move your position to either the left or right of center. After a while, you will feel completely dizzy. Then sit down and look at the hills around you. They will encircle you like horses on a merry-go-round, except that they are green and they do not end when the dizziness does. This is how one enters Qinghai.

Now take your life into your hands for a second by standing on a rock and looking out over a canyon, where there is no single sign of any person for as far as you can see or hear. This canyon exists in Qinghai. You may not believe that it exists or that it is as big as the Grand Canyon in Arizona, which is flooded by hundreds of tourists every day and has a special national park service center to make sure that you do not feed the grizzly bears or hike in places where rattlesnakes prefer to sleep during the afternoon to avoid the sun. But the canyon in Qinghai is somehow every bit as big and as deep. There are only two differences. The first is, there are no tourists, and therefore, no need for tourist hosting service centers. In fact, there are no people at all. The second is, if you try to reach high enough without falling off the rocks, you can almost touch the white eagles.

At this place, if you listen, you can only hear the wind. It eliminates other sounds in your mind, rushing through your consciousness like a rising tide which suddenly subsides, leaving waves to crash upon rocks. When you feel the white salt water breaking about, open your eyes and realize for a second that you are nowhere near the sea but standing on a cliff far above the Yellow River which runs below. The sound of waves was only an illusion. It was just the breathing of the white eagles.

Place a call on a mobile phone where a connection can still be obtained, upon a cliff where the Tibetans have left stones and prayer flags, a small *manidui*, reachable only by a hike over a thin ridge from which if you fall. There will be no return, except to be washed into the brown rich sticky mud of the Yellow River. Place a call by satellite signal and hold the phone up as high as you can in the wind. Remember not to lose your balance. Let somebody somewhere else, who will never have the opportunity to visit this canyon, listen to the wind in this place that has no people. From where they are — the glass and steel office tower — let them try to understand the reason why white eagles cry after eating fresh blood. If they hang up the phone on you, just hike on.

This brings us back to the question of the ball of string. Start to unravel it. Pull the string along with you and watch it unravel. There is a road that you can see as far as you can and when you turn your head you can only see what you have left behind for as far as you can remember. When you forget what you remembered, you may begin again. This is the paradox you will find yourself in throughout a journey down this road into the place called Qinghai. Now imagine the ball unraveling in your hand during the course of this journey. Imagine you keep pulling the string and watching the ball turn in concentric circles. As the string gets longer, the ball gets smaller. By progressing in a process toward infinity, it will eventually disappear.

Now begin the same process. Follow the road as it passes villages that are simple. In the eyes of some, they may be poor, but in the eyes of others, they are rich. Put a thumb up in the wind and hitchhike. The trucks will pass. There are only trucks on this road — large transport vehicles — blue steel iron trucks filled with horses, sheep, and people. Tibetans and Muslims, with bandannas covering their faces from sun and dirt, reveal only black eyes staring back with an empty forlorn feeling one gets from traveling for many days on a single dirt road.

The trucks pass quickly, spattering mud on your jeans. Do not mind. As far as they are concerned, you are not meant to be here, so they ignore you. Then the trucks are gone and more trucks arrive, only to pass without stopping. Keep hitchhiking in the wind and rain. As the rain clouds pass, revealing snow-capped mountains from which snows melt into water and trickle into rivers which roar in the direction you wish to proceed in. Follow the rivers and they will lead you. Listen to the sound of ice dissipating upon stone, becoming ice cold water. Then look for signs of the white eagles.

This is a place where the desert is surrounded by snow-capped distant mountains, in your mind, Shangri-La. Only in Qinghai will you see such a contrast — white snow-capped mountains which can only be reached through hiking across white dunes of sand which cannot be crossed. This means that the mountains are unreachable. No such place ever existed in your mind. So you believe it must be an illusion. You try to convince yourself about this. You will even insist, because you have run out of string.

Before reaching the sand dunes, a young Tibetan girl runs with her sheep. Behind her, her long hair is braided into a pattern of turquoise, which is her greatest material possession. She wears it in her hair while tending to her sheep. She even forgets it is there, oblivious to its weight on the back of her head. It does not bother her at all because she has already disregarded possession. As she runs quickly through the grasslands, the sheep scatter. They run in different directions.

If you dare to cross the sand dunes, cover your face with a bandanna. The sun will scorch you and make your head throb with sharp, penetrating pain. The mirage you see is only your own shadow on the cracking alkaline, which runs through the desert. This is where you come in the late afternoon to sit and watch your shadow grow, stretch into the horizon and disintegrate before you.

There are faint contours in the land that give way to more patches of grass and the sight of Tibetan nomads herding sheep. Faces covered in colorful bandannas, they are gypsies. Turquoise sewn into young women's hair trails across their shoulders. Ask them where Shangri-La is. They will laugh at you and hurry to round up more sheep before sunset. If you wait, you may be left where they left you, repeating the same question.

Cross the sand dunes. They will lead you to where you do not want to, but must go. It is part of the journey that will only end in the early morning hours when a pick-up truck brings you to a Muslim village. There, you will see the men sitting in a broken wooden shop drinking *babao* tea, which is made of rock sugar and dates. The men will talk and laugh. Piping hot lamb is served with noodles that are cut with a long wide knife. It is a Muslim village, so no liquor is served. Everyone drinks tea. A dog barks somewhere, another howls. Their cry is soon forgotten.

The pick-up truck continues. It will eventually bring you through the dark of the night to a town where you will not discover until dawn. There, you wake up on a bed above a shop house

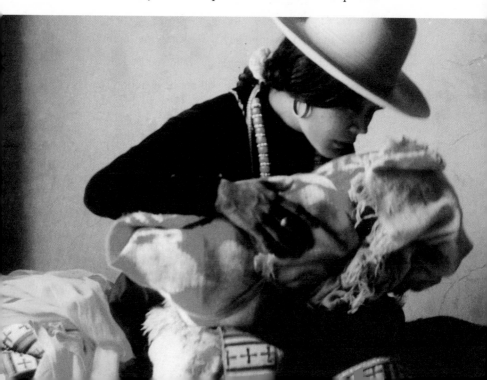

where some monks lead you in your sleep, where the truck dumps you along the road. It is a cowboy town. The Tibetans come here in boots and high hats. Some ride motorcycles. They push their way into the Muslim restaurants and order racks of fresh lamb. The lamb is killed outside, nearby. Muslims pray when they kill a lamb because its screams can be disturbing. Here, the air is cold all year. They eat a lot of lamb. Prayers of deference are continuously given.

A woman enters the restaurant as you leave. She is wrapped in blankets, a tall felt hat upon her head. She has high red-burned Tibetan cheeks, a forlorn smile of hopeless graciousness. Her hands are already tough as leather but her face is soft as the child in her hands. She pulls it close to her breast for feeding. She is young. It is her first baby. She holds this child as if it is the only thing she will ever have. It is.

Leave the restaurant. They will sweep the lamb bones onto the floor and then serve more lamb, followed by *babao* tea. More prayers will be uttered but you will not be there to listen, because you will have already entered the mountains.

The rivers lead into more mountains. There are canyons like Sedona, Bryce Canyon — places which you have passed in another lifetime in southwestern Arizona or New Mexico. The feeling of hitchhiking is the same. A truck passes, one stops. You hop in and travel to the next point of arrival, which becomes a point of departure. When you are tired from walking, you rest. The space is a sequence of layers through time. Time becomes elusive like the white eagles, flying close but never forgetting to stop. They, too, are afraid of losing their balance.

The mountains come to a place where the green becomes layers of dry earth, upon which grows sparse, long grass that stretch into planes. The planes rise in plateaus. There are ridges and layers of dirt that show disintegration by the wind. The wind was here first. You cannot keep up with it. If you try to catch it, it will behave elusively and mislead you into following dust blowing in all directions.

There are spots of alkaline on the plane, parched scabs where dryness has sucked sweet water from earth, drawing salt-like alkaline to the surface, forming flat white patches. The earth here is cracked like a jigsaw puzzle that somebody has forgotten to put together. In frustration, they left wandering off into the desert to die.

Such a sense of sudden desertion haunts the patches of alkaline. Watch your shadow in those broken pieces of flat ground. They will cause an illusion and you will believe that your entire image is a shattered mirror reflecting something that you do not want to imagine, but which has already happened and passed before you as a subconscious image. When your own image has shattered between the stark lines of the cracked alkaline earth, you will see the reflected mood of your soul. Stand up and walk away. It is time for you to walk into the desert as well.

Finding Nomads

I did not find the nomads. When time was appropriate, they found me. They knew it was the appropriate time because I had already entered the mountains.

At 4,000 meters above sea level, the road ceased to exist. It became a walking trail, then a path, then a creek. After crossing the creek, I came upon prints of horse hooves in the mud. I stepped across the mud. The creek led into a valley. There were three Tibetan pagodas in the valley with some *jingfan* tied to them. There was nothing else there. Nobody was in the valley. I meditated in front of the three white pagodas until the sun rose across the smooth white stone and mud edge. The glare reflected in the sunglasses that were intended to cut the glare. I looked into the sunglasses' inner edge and realized my shadow was making a clockwise journey around me as I sat before the three pagodas. My shadow's journey would last only until the sun set on the other side of the three pagodas. I remembered not to forget that clocks cannot be turned backwards. The pagodas were pure white.

For Tibetans, white is the color of purity. For the Chinese, it is the color of death. For some reason, white has been chosen as the color of pagodas which are often built upon the ashes of great Buddhist monks who spent their lives seeking purity, in valleys which cannot be found because nobody remembers where they had walked before or where the pagodas were built until someone walks into the valley again, searching for them. If purity can only be buried under a white pagoda, then one can wait for death to become pure. I began meditating on the color white.

My thoughts were interrupted by a nomad who was wearing a dirty blanket and riding on a horse. He laughed at me and asked where I was going. I explained that I was looking for Shangri-La. He offered me a ride.

I rode on the back of his horse and went deeper into the valley. The valley had no roads, only a horse trail formed in mud by horse hooves. It was not a deliberate path. Nobody designed or approved it or sought government funding or bank loans to build it with contractors asking for kickbacks. There were only horses passing this way, sometimes frequently, sometimes not at all. There were also sheep and yaks, herded by Tibetans riding horses. This is how the path came to be. It is a crossing remembered only by horses.

Deep in the valley, we came upon black tents that were woven out of yak fur. These tents were the homes of the nomads. We passed by a yak bull that went insane. He was dragging tent poles on his back and being herded with the other yaks. He tore apart the tent on his back, flinging poles everywhere. One might think that the bull had gone insane. On the other hand, he was just tired of being herded with other yaks.

I left the nomads and from there, I walked deeper into the valley. Deep in the valley, I came upon a Tibetan woman riding a snow-white horse. She got off the horse and spoke to me. She was curious. I asked if I could ride the horse. She gave me the reins and

I got on. The horse threw me off immediately. I pulled myself up off the damp grass and shook my head. I had not been thrown by a horse since I was a kid. As a kid, I had grown up riding horses. Perplexed, I got back on the saddle. The horse ran. He ran like crazy. I realized that he did not intend to stop. I could not stop him. The saddle slipped to the side. The strap was not tight. Or maybe, I simply lost balance. Again, I found myself on the ground, with one foot caught in the stirrup. The horse dragged me for a few moments until I slipped my foot out. He continued to run ahead in an uncertain direction. Eventually, he stopped to chomp on the grass.

The Tibetan lady ran over to me. She smiled as if nothing had happened. "You ride him!" I said, shaking the dirt off both hands angrily.

She smiled again. "He is a wild horse. I do not want to ride him either. He is very unpredictable," she said with innocence, if the horse was wild, then why did she let me ride it? I wondered. I looked into her eyes. Clearly, she had not thought about this. If I wanted to ride a wild horse, then ride him.

She had a round face. On her head was a tall, beige felt hat. Her hair was braided into thin tight braids favored by Tibetan women. "Such work takes at least four hours," she explained with pride. Turquoise and chunks of coral were braided into her hair. "These were my mother's," she touched them with a feeling of connectivity with the past. "She gave these to me. I wear them every day." Grabbing the white horse by its leather reins, she yanked him from his grass-munching. He followed reluctantly. "He is not a bad horse," she apologized, purity beaming from her black Tibetan eyes. "He is not bad at all, not like other horses. He is just wild." I was beginning to understand the meaning of the color white.

She asked me where I was going. I said, "To Shangri-La." She shrugged her shoulders with indifference and said almost as an afterthought, "I will take you. It is over there, in the next valley. This way." She led the way. We walked into the valley. Green rose to white-capped mountains. Snow had taken refuge from summer there while freeing unpossessed ice into the freezing rivers. Shadows of clouds crossed the valley and patterns of sunlight created an illusion of change as mountains stood still. In the distance, an old lady sat before her yak fur tent. She held a baby — her grandchild, into another generation, she was projecting spirit.

The Tibetan woman led her white horse, pulling the leather reins. She brought me further into the valley above the river. She stopped where the horse neighed, before a black yak fur tent. We went inside, where she introduced me to three women who were her friends. One held a baby to her breast. It snuggled from the cold within layers of bright woven cloth, suckling milk. The tent was black, but it was not dark inside. There was plenty of light. Within, one could see the outside through pores of space between woven yak fur. While insulating against rain and cold, it provided light and was almost transparent. The elements of space within filled with pungent smoke. A fire in the center of their tent exuded warmth. A pile of yak manure dried into hardened bricks beside the tent's entrance provided fuel for fire. Smoke drifted upward, mixing with a sharp blade of sunlight filtering into space from a hole directly above through which smoke escaped against crystal light into clear shrill blue air.

A white eagle flew above. He was followed by other white eagles. The women stepping from their tent pointed to the white eagles and told me that there must be wolves below the white eagles. Maybe a yak had died and would soon be consumed. One of the men came over with two boys. They had finished their morning work. Together, they sat on blankets spread upon grass. The women sat kneeling beside them. One boy played a Tibetan mandolin. It was the sound of three strings in a valley surrounded by snow-capped mountains. We were the only ones in the valley with the sound of three strings. The man began chanting. His voice called like an echo, rising as spirit, becoming thunder of wild horses running in uncertain directions. I listened in silence. He chanted. Together, we watched the white eagles.

Yak Milk Cheese

A monk wandered across the river into the valley. I did not know where he came from or when he joined us until I noticed he was there. Maybe I had not been looking carefully enough. Maybe it had something to do with the way Tibetan monks arrive. They do not arrive. They appear.

He appeared in saffron robes, head shaven except for a small mustache and goatee. Smiling like an elf, he sat beside us and asked, "Where are you going?"

"I am searching for Shangri-La. Do you know where it is? What direction should I go in?"

His smile widened over his goatee stretching to pointed elf ears. With a flourish of his hand he offered to lead the way, into another valley narrower than the one we were in. A snow peak hovered over the crest of the mountain above us. A freezing cold river ran before us. We followed the river, then crossed it. Like an oasis in contrast, a tiny factory building stood before us across the river. We crossed upon the stones as there was no bridge. The stones had been rounded by the freezing water. They were cold too. The Tibetan woman leading a white horse followed.

The workers, surprised by our sudden arrival, stepped from the factory to greet us. Among them was a saffron-robed monk, who introduced himself as head of the factory. I was to discover shortly he was head of an entire monastery as well.

"Factory?" I was shocked. "There is a factory here? What are you producing in the factory?"

"Cheese," explained the monk.

"Cheese?"

"Yes, cheese."

"How can you make cheese in a factory away from everything and everywhere that is here?"

"We make yak milk cheese. We need to be near the yaks."

I thought for a moment as yak butter tea was poured before me by the Tibetan woman in a beige hat, whose white horse was now chomping grass. The monk running this factory was named Jigme Jensen. Within the next day or so, he would not only change the way I think about cheese, but also about business models and relationships between mountains, rivers, people, yaks and education. I asked about yak milk cheese. He showed me his factory.

There were only three large rooms. But before we entered the rooms, Jigme asked me to put on rubber boots and a white medic jacket and facemask, as if I was entering an operating room. "We must keep international health standards here when making yak cheese for export," Jigme explained with a flourish of his hand as if he was about to wipe Dutch Gouda off the market. Sure enough, upon entering the factory, I could have stepped into a cheese factory outside Amsterdam. The same techniques were applied — yak milk churned in heated vats, settling into moulds, solidifying into cheese stored on wooden racks in cool rooms, I was convinced

Jigme Jensen was making cheese. Only one question remained. "Why here?"

"Because we need to be close to the nomads who bring us fresh yak milk every morning and every evening through this door," Jigme pointed to a side door leading to the room with big hot churning vats.

"But you are nowhere near any point of distribution," I queried. There were no roads or point of connection. We were in the middle of nomad country in mountains within the heart of a "green sea". "If you want to sell your cheese internationally, or even in China, you have to be manufacturing closer to infrastructure and distribution points," I volunteered the professional advice of a lawyer and business advisor.

"You see, I don't worry about distribution," Jigme was not interested in the urban advice I carried in my baggage. "I do not want to manufacture cheese in a place which might be inconvenient for nomads," he explained. "You see, I am manufacturing yak cheese."

"It still did not make sense. So what if you are making yak cheese in yak country? How do you get the cheese to the market? " He still hadn't answered my question. "Excuse me, but it does not make any commercial sense to build a factory here just to provide convenience to nomads making yak milk deliveries."

"But that's just the point," Jigme insisted. "You see, they all live in mountains, in yak felt tents at high altitudes. They cannot leave the valleys so easily. So by having the factory here in the mountains, they can deliver yak milk every day, even twice a day.

This way, the milk is assured to be fresh."

I still did not understand this. "You can raise yaks on farms near a factory near a city or point of distribution, right?"

"Wrong. It would not be wild yak milk," Jigme sighed, "that is milk from yaks herded by nomads. My real purpose is to help nomads."

Now I understood. Jigme Jensen explained that he had obtained investment from the Trace Foundation, established by Andrea Soros, daughter of George Soros. Jigme used funds she donated to build the cheese factory in nomad country. The nomads traditionally had no income. Now, without affecting their traditional lifestyle, Jigme was providing income by purchasing yak milk every day. In fact, he was not changing their traditional means of livelihood but supporting it.

The hardship of distributing cheese from this isolated factory was Jigme's problem to overcome. Every day, he would fill up a jeep with round cheese blocks and drive through mud and rivers out of mountains to the nearest cowboy town. Then along that long winding road to Xining, from which yak milk cheese would be exported to Europe and North America, becoming the most exotic cocktail party contraption one could offer within chic wine-tasting circles. Meanwhile, nomads had income while keeping their traditional lifestyle intact. They continued to herd yak, live in yak tents and ride wild white horses.

Jigme explained that since establishing the cheese factory, nomad income in the surrounding valleys and mountains had increased without affecting their lifestyle.

My question to Jigme was how to re-invest his own profits? Expand the cheese factory?

"No." Jigme explained that he had other ideas. He was about to build another school.

"Another school?"

"Yes, another school."

"Where? Here?"

"No. There." He pointed in a direction. "In the next valley, which is the valley after that next valley below that other valley. Yes, the one over there. Do you understand? Yes, over there." Jigme pointed in an uncertain direction. "Would you like to see? I must go there tomorrow to determine the plot lines for the walls of the school. After I determine which line should go in which direction, we will begin to build it with money we obtain from selling yak milk cheese to the world." I was beginning to understand Jigme's economic model for globalization of yak milk cheese. But I did not understand this thing about a school.

The next morning, we rose early to the sound of nomads delivering fresh yak milk to the factory's side door. The sound of pony hooves crushing dew dripping grassland had already evaporated from my mind as I rubbed my eyes. I stepped from the tent Jigme had pitched for me outside the factory, washed my face in the river below and wandered back. The nomads had left. "They come early to deliver yak's milk," Jigme explained. "Afterwards, they return to the mountains."

Yak butter tea was poured into a bowl with *zamba*, a muesli-looking wheat cereal. Jigme encouraged me to let yak butter tea absorb the *zamba*. Soon the yak butter tea had been absorbed by the cereal which became a pasty, sticky wheat pastry, something like a soft granola bar. I remembered to look carefully when looking for Shangri-La in a cup of yak butter tea filled with *zamba*.

"This is *zamba*," explained Jigme. "We Tibetans eat it for breakfast, lunch and sometimes for dinner. *Zamba* is the basic staple at all Tibetan meals."

"You know, this tastes like muesli, a Western-style cereal. I think you could export this with the cheese," I suggested. "It would go over real well with all the New Age health types and in organic food stores. That's a great name too, highly marketable with that crowd. It would be a hit in California. Just call it '*Zamba*'."

"I have already registered the '*Zamba*' trademark," Jigme nodded.

With a flourish of his saffron robe, Jigme led me into his jeep driven by another monk. Jigme sat in front and I sat squeezed in between two other monks in the back. I was the only one not wearing saffron. We bounced down the narrow trail driving through rivers, balancing across collapsing ridges. Eventually, we followed a river into a valley, then into another valley. Jigme pointed excitedly out the window. "See that tent in the distance. There are two young children in that nomad family, both girls. Do you see that tent there?" he pointed in another direction. I could barely see a tent on the horizon surrounded by tiny dots — yaks. "There are several more girls living there. None of them has any opportunity to go to school because they are nomads living here in mountains. I will bring the school to them. They will be my students."

We drove into another valley, and sure enough, several workers were there painting wall lines of what would be a school on rounding, flattening portion of grassland. Jigme jumped out of the jeep and strode over to them, arguing over where the lines should be drawn to make more room for the classrooms. He looked more like a construction site boss than a monk. The line was adjusted. The classroom would be a bit bigger.

Rising above the valley was a sharp mountain, its surface cliff. Jigme broke his attention away from questions of building foundation to point at the cliff. Small dots could be seen at a point two-thirds up to the top. "There are caves there," he whispered. "Monks used to come to this place for meditation. It is a good location for a school."

Still I was perplexed. "But why don't you build the school closer to town? The children can go there and stay in a dorm. Return to their parents on holiday. It would be so much easier."

"You see, their parents all live in the mountains, in yak felt tents at high altitudes. They cannot leave the valleys so easily. So by having the school here in mountains, they can go to school every day and then go home to be with their parents twice a day. Their traditional lifestyle will not be affected. I do not want to build a school in a place which might be inconvenient for the nomads."

"What will the school be like?"

Jigme waved me back into the jeep. We drove up the hill along a ridge crest, following a path without any road. The driver was following his instincts. The entrance to this valley would lead to a river that would lead out from another valley. Within a matter of hours, we had left the mountains. We arrived back to the cowboy town I had crashed in just a day or two before. It somehow seemed like a long time ago, as if time had been lost in valleys and mountains.

We drove through the cowboy town. Tibetan cowboys in big hats riding motorcycles were still riding back and forth as if it was the same movie I had watched several days ago, except that John Wayne was not in it, the Muslims had kept a monopoly on lamb shanks and the Navahos had become Tibetans. Whoosh ... the doors of a small restaurant spun open as a Tibetan in sharp cowboy boots, tall hat and big plastic sunglasses pushed his way into the street standing off sharply in front of another Tibetan. He gave him a tough look in the eye, then swinging onto his heavy metal motorcycle, he rode off into the sunset, leaving only a stream of dust settling behind.

Jigme was oblivious to all this and signaled to his driver who sped through the little town toward a gate which was opened by other monks. We entered. Before me was a Tibetan-style building beautifully constructed of stone and wood with fresh bright paintings of colorful horses, monkeys and elephants. A monk unlocked the clean glass doors and nodded in deference as Jigme explained that it was summer break, so all the students had gone home to their parents. He invited me in.

On the first floor, Jigme led me into a physics lab full of modern equipment, then into a chemistry lab, I followed him down the hallway — colorful Tibetan paintings on the walls — into a small library. It was filled with both Chinese and Tibetan books. There were copies of sacred text written on traditional long Tibetan paper in a cabinet. There were also copies of American books, even Disney cartoons for kids. "Tibetan children like Mickey Mouse," Jigme noted as he led me upstairs.

On the second, top floor of this little school we entered classrooms filled with computers, the latest Internet equipment, putting Qinghai online. Jigme then turned on a computer and showed me how the written Tibetan language is now digitized, used for Internet communication throughout the greater Qinghai-Tibetan Plateau. Jigme explained that his school was offering nomad children 24-hour global Internet access for free. "They can come into these rooms after school and go online. We encourage that. They can be connected to the world from our little school in Qinghai."

Jigme Jensen went on to explain, "It is the first private school in this region, meaning we have had no government funding support. When they say they support something, it is only in words, not in substance. So we did it on our own. Our school welcomes any nomad children, regardless of ethnicity or religion. We have Tibetans, Muslims and Manchurians. At our school, education is free. It is all paid for with cheese."

Meditation

As we left the school, Jigme and I walked along the Yellow River. Brown and gold glistened across its flat surface in the morning sun against the banks of red soil washed flat by the river known throughout history as 'China's Sorrow'. "Yes, this is the Yellow River, the mother river of all Chinese," Jigme said. "The Yellow River's origin is here, Ma Duo County. Travel along the river. After two large bends in the river, from this spot, you will come to its origin. According to the landscape of Buddhism, this curve in the river before our monastery is a very good place. Our ancestors chose to build Lajia Monastery here because this is the best place." He led me to the monastery.

Inside Lajia Monastery is a temple. We entered the temple. We walked past rows of candles. I followed Jigme Jensen. Candles led through the darkness, which became light when he held aloft a tiny brass cup of yak butter oil. A burning light flickered, eating oil on the surface of the yak butter. Rows of candles on all sides of this temple barely illuminated the *thankas* and statues of Buddha, Teachers, Bodhisattvas and Guardians. Flames floated delicately upon clear surface of yak butter that was carefully placed in each brass cup by monks in the early morning before they recite the mantra. They flickered gently as we walked past, a response to the presence of two people that were passing a flame without noticing its presence.

"Now we say this whole Qinghai-Tibetan Plateau is Shangri-La," Jigme Jensen explained, "but Shangri-La is not only one spot. The city where the future Maitreya Buddha resides is called Shangri-La. It is also Xiang Ba, which means 'kind mother'. People who do good things can find Shangri-La. Shangri-La refers to you reaching the level where the Buddha reaches."

Jigme then led me up a path behind the temple. The path rose to a point within the shadow of the sharp cliffs that reached upward to the clear blue above, touched only by the passing of white clouds, which soon dispersed. "The 9th Panchen Lama came here and stayed in this temple," Jigme explained. "There is a Panchen Palace on the hillside above this temple." He pointed to the palace, now a decaying adobe. "It is a place cultivated by a lama, and is clearly a good place. The lama had long left. The place left untouched had presence."

"The whole Qinghai-Tibetan Plateau can be called Shangri-La," Jigme said. "People here are close to Buddhism since their birth. Therefore, their hearts are kind. Compare with some polluted big cities, the place without pollution can be called Shangri-La but it is not the real Shangri-La. I have these poor students and I give them the opportunity to study, it can be said that I am doing a good thing, something that other people should also do. The most basic way to find Shangri-La is to have a good heart and be giving to others." Jigme went on to explain, "According to your route, you have already found many Shangri-Las. But to find the real Shangri-La, you must do things from your heart. Through doing good things for others, you can find the real Shangri-La."

A dry dusty path weaves between buildings made of mud, brick, adobe, casabas of compartments in the beehive of Lajia Monastery. Monks in saffron robes walked past, oblivious to the dust. It whirls in concentric circles and settles where nobody bothers to look. "But why was the Lajia Temple built here?" I asked. Is it because of a bend in the Yellow River that is near, but still not at the source of the river? Why did the 9th Panchen Lama choose to come to this isolated place, to stay in the Lajia Temple? Why had Jigme Jensen become a Bodhisattva in disguise, bringing education to children of nomads who had been forgotten by the rest of the world? I was curious, and asked Jigme to tell me more.

He said nothing but brought me to a hillside above Lajia Temple, beside altars where pine branches were burned as incense, the final point before sheer cliffs rose above the monastery. Energy emanates from the cliffs. Below aeries of white eagles, there are caves in the cliffs. Monks have come to these caves to meditate for centuries, till today. Once, over 40 monks meditated in these caves at the same time, creating a compact space of concentration between the realm of the white eagles and the flow of a long winding river reflecting clouds passing in the sky. Jigme told me to sit cross-legged on this spot, beside the altars of pine incense, for a prolonged period of time to meditate.

Meditation concentrates concentration. It can bring one to his most central point of being — one's self without self. It is a process of arrival and departure without leaving or asking too specifically where you have just come from or where you will go next.

Concentration is focused on the mantra, the prayer of giving and death, a call to the white eagles encircling above. Acutely aware of all which pass below, they too can hear mantra uttered in the most elemental realm of your own subconscious.

Pine incense is lost in wind between cliffs, where 40 monks once meditated in silence, but have now gone their own way. If you think that you have heard their breathing in the wind, it is only an illusion, in fact, they were long gone. Their flesh had already been eaten by the white eagles. The white eagles too had flown to lost aeries only to die and be forgotten. Their feathers dispersed in the wind. So all you can hear is the sound of your own meditation. It is the silence of concentration between deep breaths.

Sound of Snow Melting

They pray to sun,
fire necessity life philosophy.
If your dream is fire,
you can understand the
rationale of burning mist.

Misty valleys, cold rivers rush,
along ancient stone alleys
villages soon forgotten only
remembered by water sound in
an empty cup of tea.

Before snow mountains
stop, wait, listen
to melting snow sounds
echo children's chanting,
call from wilderness is a purple moon,
crying in the rain.

Yunnan

Alternative Space

Kunming on a rainy morning, rain trickles in grey shadows along tree-lined streets. The old Kunming of two-story natural wood and grey tile houses I remembered from years ago was now gone. On all sides around me, concrete slabs with blue glass stretched to the sky. Aside from the old trees, there was nothing of old Kunming left. I saw my shadow of twenty years ago, a student with a backpack, wandering among old buildings, buying French baguettes and black coffee of yesterday's Kunming. My memories vanished as black rain turned to greyish mist.

I followed an address given to me by my friend, Cheng Xindong, who divided his time between Beijing and Paris. Xindong represents the artists. Xindong believed in the expressive power of China's upcoming artists. He saw in Beijing's art circles the emergence of salons as in Paris during another era, a fusion of creative people's collective imagination giving birth to an entire milieu of art. He could see this happening because he had the perspective of someone who was born in China and who had lived for a long time in Paris. It was this historic glance which gave him perspective. So he had brought the artists together, one after another, to hold exhibitions in his old courtyard home in Beijing. Inviting ambassadors and businessmen, his home became a Paris art salon in old Beijing, becoming a platform on which they present their art to Paris and the international stage. Now, Beijing municipal government has threatened to tear down his courtyard home to make way for more cement and blue glass. Meanwhile, Beijing's artists had all fled to Kunming. There was no inspiration left in Beijing, only cement and traffic. They were all going southwest, as far from the center as possible. They were trying to escape the cement and traffic. Maybe they were searching for Shangri-La. Maybe they were all just fed up.

"Yunnan has become China's center of alternative culture. Artists and intellectuals are now gathering there. It is a focal point of new ideas and creativity," Xindong had explained to me back

in Beijing. The momentum of such a movement had to be put into context, he noted. "The history of Yunnan is fusion. From our point of view, Yunnan was historically borderland, where troops banished people and prisoners to. Han culture had to cross mountains to get there. Due to its isolation, pure culture of ethnic minority tribes has persisted there. Because of Yunnan's multi-ethnicity, people there have a more open thinking, unlike in Beijing and Shanghai. Beijing was the ancient capital — the emperor's political epicenter — so a mainstream culture emanates from there. Shanghai has historically been China's open port to the West, and yes, Western ideas come into Shanghai easily, but these are all of a commercial nature which is what drives the place. Yunnan is different."

Xindong encouraged me to go to Yunnan. I first visited the province in the early 1980s when it was a backwater and it was not an easy place to trek through. I had not been back for a decade. Now, it was the happening art scene. "It is where people go to get away from the mainstream, from commerce." Xindong suggested I meet with some of his artist friends there who are living in converted warehouses. "By the very nature of its environment, its isolation and multi-ethnicity, it is the borderland," he explained, scratching a few addresses and mobile phone numbers of artists on a piece of paper. He handed me the paper. "This is where you go to find the alternative."

I found the alternative in an alleyway behind a set of factory warehouses at an address given to me by Xindong. These factory warehouses had been turned into art galleries and studios. Beside studios and in between alleyways which split off from other main alleyways, and in places wide enough for stray cats to jump headlong down from a drainage pipe into an open trash can and to make the jump like an acrobat without spilling trash laterally across the tiny existing space between broken brick walls, tiny cafés and wine bars had opened. They became a subterfuge oasis for artists in need of an afternoon caffeine injection or a non-hallucinatory wind-down between excessive paint inhalation from abstract expression of one's inner emotions or external frustrations. I got off a public bus and found the alleyway. There, I found an artist, Ye Yongqing, sipping a double café latte with a look of contemplation on his face as if he were anticipating from which direction the stray cat above would jump in order to not miss the soft cushion of garbage in an open trash can. I sat with him and joined in the process of contemplating a stray cat's late afternoon acrobatics — a lesson in balance.

The space we sat in was actually a narrow alley with factory warehouses on each side. The factories had collapsed and gone bust because they were run according to state plans that did not fit in with the new market economy. Ye Yongqing had found it when he got sick of all the noise and bulldozing in Beijing, and came to Yunnan in search of quiet chunks of space to sit in and paint. Then, other artists came. They rented the collapsing warehouses from the factories. They renovated them, turning these cavernous rooms into studios. Then hip restaurateurs came to open chic eateries, wine bars and cafés. Every night, the factory warehouses and

alleyways buzzed with life, laughter and new ideas until sunrise. By noontime, the artists were waking up again, painting and receiving foreign agents and dealers. The most run-down factory neighborhood space had become transformed into the hottest, most expensive, second-hand rental commercial real estate in town, under the noses of state-owned enterprise managers who could still not figure out what was happening with their bankrupt factory warehouses. As I sat in the espresso alleyway chatting with Ye, I noticed some photos framed on a brick wall behind him.

"Where are those photos from?" I asked.

"They are from an artist who lives in Beijing," Ye explained. "He divides his time between Beijing and Dali, and has a special interest in local children there. These are his newest photos, of countryside children. They may lack the material possessions of city kids, but inside, they are very happy. Look at their faces. You can tell."

"What they lack in material, they make up in spiritual."

"He also did some TV stuff at the same time, those small children were very curious about this kind of modern media equipment. The teachers all told them that they must not touch them because they are very expensive and their family could not afford to pay for them if they are broken, even if they spent their whole life working just to do so. But these kids are very happy. So you have to ask yourself why so many artists are now coming to Dali from Beijing to set up work studios. They discovered they can still enjoy life doing things they like without having to spend all their time thinking and talking about making money."

"Is that the reason why so many artists are coming to Yunnan? What is the real reason? "

"In the present environment, artists have become nomads; they move around various cultures. They can live in different cultures and experiment with different ideas simultaneously. In this free state of mind, they are searching for a lifestyle which will fit them. There are many European artists who find themselves in a similar situation. For example, artists who might be living in Germany would also have a studio in Italy or Paris — a division of their life. This kind of geographic nomadic behavior brings a broader perspective over one culture. This tells us that when one searches for his soul, he must walk a very long road. It is like you now walking on this road, searching for Shangri-La."

He then took a sip from his coffee cup and thought about what he was saying. He thought for a moment longer than one might expect, but it seemed like seconds before he lifted up his head. I wondered if he had found Shangri-La in his cup of café latte. He seemed to be looking carefully enough. "Actually to me, searching for Shangri-La is like searching for a road home. We do not need to prove what Hilton described in his book. People are constantly trying to find Hilton's Shangri-La excavated in a piece of wood or a piece of grass. Shangri-La can be excavated around everybody. This generation of ours over the past 20 years have constantly sought a free and open environment, which in turn has brought us into contact with a variety of different cultures. Cultural integration is an open process. Meanwhile, we look back to our Chinese tradition. Regardless of whether you are looking back to your own tradition or integrating other cultures, that is not the point. The purpose is to go back to your own daily life and ask how you live your everyday life, to go back to find everybody's real life. Why have different artists from different places come to Kunming? They are coming for one reason alone — to open up their minds and change their everyday life."

"It seems to me that you are not only providing an environment here for painting and creating, but also for incorporating art work into life, into an alternative, or maybe, a more real lifestyle?" I asked, "Is that what's happening?"

"Correct, this is the most important and most basic thing taking place here. I have also seen many similar kinds of places. Artists always remain at a distance from society. We call this alternative life, the idea of living at the fringe of society. The things artists want to do are always pushed aside by mainstream society, so artists hang themselves in the air, and in turn, they cannot land. So how do we let them land safely on the ground? Artists should set themselves against the public. So this environment here is not like a Western functioning gallery or a pure art center, which operates on a set of business principles; a model. It in fact is neither, but can be either, it is an unstable system, but this unstable system may be more active and alive, holding out a variety of possibilities, real lifestyles that are easier to approach. It is real."

I thought about what Ye was saying, it was true. Western art galleries operate on the basis of an economic model — artist, agent, gallery, collector — all integrated into a fixed system of mainstream recognition driven by the commercially driven media. Room for the alternative does not really exist outside of defined boundaries of what should be alternative, meaning that what is chic is in fact the mainstream. Alternative writers and artists are destined to sit between trash cans in a city street and beg to support their creativity as the mainstream determines what should be creative and what should not. In fact, in mainstream society, those who determine what recognized art should be have no creativity as it is purely business to them.

"Western art galleries have a system," explained Ye. "This system does not exist in China. All third world countries lack it. I have traveled through many different countries over the past few years and frankly found the third world art scene much more exciting than what was happening in Europe or the US. I felt closer to them. These countries have no art galleries, no so-called 'contemporary art professional system'. What does art mean to those people? I have been considering this question a lot. In their lives, what are the methods people use to approach art? They in fact live in what we call alternative space, and this alternative space has provided a new model. It combines the traditional and the modern, the professional and the folk, merged together with some outstanding intellectual ideas. What they produce are full of creative energy because they actually relate to what we are discussing — a spiritually and not materially driven force."

"So could we say that it is a quest for the spiritual in escaping the material which has led so many of the art circles here in search of Shangri-La?"

"It is certain that some artists came here because of their interest in Tibetan culture. All artists have some Tibetan culture in their hearts. Not long ago, a Hong Kong magazine *Ming Bao* undertook an investigative search for Shangri-La. The journalists started from Kunming, went to Dali, then Lijiang, Jianchuan, Zhongdian and eventually arrived in Nujiang. This road, which leads to the Tibetan area, is what we called 'the road of art ecology'. There are many artists scattered on this road. They are from Beijing, Guangzhou, Taiwan and even American artists or Japanese artists went there as well. The ones who have money will buy a house; those who do not will rent a place. They run bars and just live there. There are also people like us, like migratory birds, who do not buy a house, but come here every year to get together with these people, to feel the mountains, the rivers, the sky, the earth, to hike and to enjoy a different scenery."

"Then this must be the road to Shangri-La, right?"

"It is neither right nor wrong. Everybody is searching for Shangri-La in their own way. It is not important for us, in fact. You do not have to look for it purposely. However, it is related to these landforms and this route. All these routes, to me, mean friends. There are people who love their lives. Of course, there are mountains, rivers, sky and earth which move you too. The most important are human feelings, history and your memories of it. Kunming is my hometown, but like all cities in China, is changing very fast. All modern cities in China have been changed such that they have no more history, no character, no tradition — faceless without a meaningful lifestyle — they all became the same. How can this kind of cities keep people and retain memories without human feelings? We ordinary people have lost the things we loved, but we were not able to change it. We can only go back to our small environment to create a homeland of our own and add our love to it. Like those artists we just visited in the lofts upstairs, they are building and creating their own lives. Living inside, they find and bring back a so-called Shangri-La, bit by bit."

"So there is no road to Shangri-La?"

Ye Yongqing thought for a moment. He stared into his empty cup of café latte, as if he was searching for something which may not be there. He stared. The cup was empty. I knew he was searching carefully. "Artists devote all their lives to creating different works, but work is not purpose. This work is also the artist in search of his own life's process, it is also a part of his life," he explained. "Without this kind of life, he cannot create this kind of work. Without creating this kind of work, he will not dream of this kind of life. Searching for Shangri-La is a process. You are always in the process of searching for it."

When I left the alleyway which had become the space of artists, in the process of seeking something which could be called Shangri-La, if you searched for it long enough in a cup of café latte, I noticed an old broken sofa on top of one of the buildings. As I began to hitchhike down the road, I thought about the lonely sofa on top of the broken warehouse which had now become the most expensive property in Kunming because artists were turning around disregarded space into a realm of creative energy.

I thought about the energy, then that sofa and wondered to myself which artist might occupy it each day, sitting on it to reflect between painting sessions. How he would be feeling between the rip in his torn blue jeans, the pain of the sharp decrepit springs piercing through a ragged sofa cover. He would be staring at the pigeons flying above between the lofts of the warehouses. They could be white eagles on a vast Tibetan plain, if one closed their eyes long enough to reflect within the black sensation created by blindfolding and pretending to turn off all the lights in the studio loft, walking around without any clothes on for five minutes. In moments like this, one can arrive at a specific point of clarity. It is sometimes called "alternative space".

No One Listens

I hitchhiked down the road outside Kunming. New highways were being built over what was once red clay earth. I thought that new highways would be very convenient for motorists in the future. Certainly there would be a lot more cars in Kunming in the future. I thought how convenient it would be. Then, I thought how I would miss the red clay under my feet.

Yunnan means "south of the clouds". Beneath the clouds is red clay, which ethnic minorities of Yunnan have carved with their hands across millennium into rice and coffee terraces. If you flew in a low plane or took enough hallucinations to believe that you were flying somewhere between the clouds and a land of clay, you could see in this spectrum of sun and rain which in convergence is the south, the level plateaus, terraces carved by hand by those who still care for clay. In the sunlight after the rain, they become a spectrum of colors. This is caused by the contraction of sunlight touching a thin water surface that rests between banks of soft dirt and red clay beneath.

As the truck dumped me off, I walked across a tread-run dirt road and found myself standing before high clay walls. This was the address that Xindong in Beijing had given me. He said I would come to a place that was not really a place because it could only be identified by high clay walls. When I found these walls, I would find Luo Xu's studio. Luo Xu had spent his entire life working with clay. He had done so as an artist, and before that, as a construction worker. During the "Cultural Revolution", he had to dig mud. So when I found high walls which were not made of cement and covered in bathroom tiles and blue glass of every single building in China being developed by either government or developers, but rather, a wall made of just soft, reddish, brownish, and yellowish hardened clay, I knew I had come to the right place — Luo Xu's studio.

I found Luo Xu living behind the high walls surrounding his studio. Behind the walls was a beat-up car from the 1950s, the type used by Stalin or other communist leaders, covered with a hallucination of spray paint colors. Inside the compound was a garden, with wild flowers growing uncontained. Vast and seemingly beehive structures dominated the garden. Each was constructed of clay bricks. I was to discover that these were catacomb structures built by Luo Xu to permanently display his art. In each catacomb stood towering figures — legs of women interwoven creating huge terrifying insect images, clay torsos and bodies in positions of pleasure and pain. And everywhere, one could see Luo Xu's trademark heads, ceramic extended necks with heads, open mouths laughing, screaming and crying. The heads were stacked together like crowds in a city, going to work, jammed on a lunch break, leaving work, but never leaving the city.

I had seen all the museums in New York, Paris, London, Amsterdam and Barcelona, but never had I seen such a creative, ingenious museum — the huge beehive catacombs single-handedly constructed out of brick from his own kiln by Luo Xu. But this was not an art gallery or a museum. People were not invited to come to see Luo Xu's art. In fact, he did not want to be bothered by people at all. He was purposely displaying art for nobody to see at all.

"How long ago did you move here to establish your studio?" I asked.

"About 6 to 7 years ago," he thought for a moment, sitting cross-legged on a Chinese stool. He poured some tea and lit a cigarette, which put him in the mood to think. After thinking for a while, he added, almost as an afterthought, "I came here in 1995."

"I can see that not many people visit your place now," I said out loud without thinking. Only a lone donkey, which Luo Xu kept as his "friend", stood in the garden. The donkey had full reign over Luo Xu's space. He would eat some wild flowers, walk among the talking or screaming heads, and sometimes nudge Luo Xu, who affectionately pet the donkey's short fur on the flat area between its eyes. "Maybe you do not like them visiting here," I thought more clearly. "Is that correct?"

"I am not a very 'social' person. I cannot be calm with too many annoying people around. However, if someone can bring something of interest to me, I can sacrifice a bit of time. The problem is that people normally bring nothing to me except noise. I have no interest in noise."

"A lot of people are trying to escape noise nowadays. Many Beijing artists are coming to Yunnan, seeking a quiet, calm environment away from the big, busy city life," I took a sip of tea.

The donkey nudged his nose into my cup.

"In our history, Yunnan was lost in the high mountains, far away from the emperors," Luo Xu explained. "So for thousands of years, the emperors really did not know what was happening in Yunnan. The court in Beijing only knew there was a place called Yunnan, which was a part of the empire. For centuries, it was isolated and depended entirely on itself. In the olden days, the emperors banished those Chinese that they did not like to Yunnan because it was considered a wilderness, a distant outpost. Many of the ethnic Chinese here today are descendants of those left over from then. At that time, there were only ethnic minorities in Yunnan, each with their own small kingdoms, lots of what we call in Chinese, '*tu huang di*' — the 'local dirt emperors' — who were basically warlords. To a great extent, the psychological framework of that time persists today. There is a big difference between Yunnan and the rest of China." In these words, Luo Xu explained why so many artists were congregating in Yunnan, each in a way banished by the mainstream, seeking distance from the center, escaping all the noise.

The donkey began wandering toward at an old Yunnan-styled courtyard home, which had been re-assembled and restored on one corner of the property. "Luo Xu, is that your old house?" I asked, pointing at the courtyard.

"Yes. When my hometown started what they called 'city construction', they wanted to destroy it. I brought it here and restored it. Now the entire old town is destroyed, everything torn down. At that time, I felt terrible. I did not have the means or capital to save more houses. I really wanted to keep them all, move them to another place to keep them. There were many very grand, old houses. This one was just an ordinary one."

"Of the entire ancient town, at least you were able to save this one house, while some developers and corrupted officials were busy destroying the rest. This is happening all over China," I pointed out. "Look at Beijing. They have literally obliterated the city's heritage."

"I think Chinese people are very interesting," Luo Xu sighed, drinking his tea, one eye thoughtfully watching his donkey chewing wild flowers as it gradually moved closer to his old restored home. "A powerful energy lies hiding within them," Luo explained. "If there is a direction, everybody will follow. The situation is like when Chairman Mao waved his hand, everybody would start to destroy things, start to criticize their own parents. This aspect of Chinese people's energy is quite terrible. However, it is still growing. Maybe many years later, by the next generation or the generation after that, there will be an explosion of energy among the young people who will tear down all the architecture of the 1980s and 1990s. This energy will make the whole country crazy, which is a very interesting characteristic of Chinese people. Look at the classic architecture of old Beijing, and even Kunming. This energy allows them to tear down both the good and the bad. In their eyes, this old architecture is poor and backwards. One day, when the future generation sees what we have now, they may dismantle all these houses too. It is quite possible. China's several thousands of years of mass movements have witnessed this kind of terrible thing, especially in modern times. Today, you have tired people and wasted money. They only know how to dismantle one thing and put up another thing. They do not know how to use it, protect it and feel for it. In my mind, the past architecture and culture are like my parents. Think of an old man. No matter how senile this old man may be, he is your parent. The old house is the same. Despite the lack of modern conveniences, it is still your parent. You cannot kick out your parents because they are old. Nowadays, people tear down old houses just like kicking out their old parents, thinking they are old and ugly, a burden. In fact, an old man sitting there quietly does not disturb anybody. He is just sitting there happily and quietly, he does not disturb you, and moreover, he brought you up."

Luo Xu pointed out that Chinese culture always promoted respect for elderly people, taking care of small children, and respecting parents, in turn, he could not understand the rapid and accelerating erosion of such values over the recent years. Maybe it was caused by the wild rush to become Westernized. Maybe it was caused by a newfound love of money and all the things it can buy. "You dislike and look down on these old houses," he said of developers and local officials alike. "You want to decorate yourself like a rich European family, not like a Chinese farmer, an old man who lives in an old house. The old house has natural flowers and grass growing around it. There are birds flying freely in the sky and animals running in the woods. The roots of all these things are the same. They are living together. In fact, they are in harmony. Now, some cultural and economic phenomena violates the basic rule that many things must live together to survive in this world, which makes the world interesting. The new rule is to only allow one thing to exist, but seeking only one thing is too simple. China, for the past few years, has been crazily using porcelain tiles to smother all the new concrete buildings in them. This is a big joke. The demand for porcelain tiles in China must be the greatest in the world."

Luo Xu was referring to the phenomena of old historic buildings being torn down by developers, only to be replaced by cement blobs covered with bathroom tiles. Such structures were the standards. You can drive through almost any city or town in China and see them everywhere, one building after another, all the same, covered with bathroom tiles and blue glass. "In foreigners' eyes, these kind of white porcelain tiles are used to decorate toilets," I pointed out. Yes, it seemed to many foreign observers that China's urban planners, while obliterating their nation's architectural heritage, had in Freudian terms an infatuation with designing building exteriors to look like public restroom interiors. "This kind of thing represents the current mood in China, blindly copying Western things without understanding what they are all about."

"China is trying its best to learn from the West. Hong Kong has learned from the West. So China thinks Hong Kong is the closest to the West, so they learn everything from Hong Kong. I have thought about this, as with anything. First, you have to have a feeling about it, and be familiar with it. It is like a bird building its little nest. It is built very scientifically because a bird is very familiar with a piece of rattan and how to use sticky dirt. The reason is, it deals with these elements everyday. So we can see a nest done casually and elegantly because the bird is so familiar with the elements it uses. Unfamiliarity means it has no feelings for something, so it can only admire it blindly. The unfamiliar image will not fit you. Western people have been using steel and cement for many years. It took so many years in Europe to create modern architecture in the context of their history and cultural changes. They are very familiar with these elements of theirs. They have feelings for it. Do Chinese people have such feelings? Over the course of thousands of years of Chinese history, we Chinese people have slept with wood and bricks. Ask yourself, how come we have the Forbidden City? There is no Forbidden City in Europe. Likewise, there are no good modern cities in China." Luo Xu leaned over. His donkey was strolling back for more attention. He began petting the donkey on its forehead between its eyes. Its ears perked. "Any animal knows why it needs to grow a certain color of fur because it has gone through several thousand years of evolution. It is just as if I suddenly changed the color of my skin. I will still not be like white people. A flower is a flower; a tiger is a tiger."

Luo Xu then asked me why I had come to Yunnan to hang out with artists. I explained that I had started my trip in Lhasa, hanging out with monks, traveling through Qinghai with the nomads. He understood, nodded and lit another cigarette. I explained, "Not only Chinese artists, but a lot of foreigners are getting fed up with the fatigue of urban values. They too, are escaping to quiet places in western China, searching for Shangri-La."

"This is a current direction. A trend. However," he sipped his tea, petting his donkey, "I think differently. Actually, a quiet place can be found anywhere. I think quiet places can be found in cities too. Of course, this requires seeking energy within oneself." Luo Xu observed three kinds of Shangri-La seekers. "There are many big-shot city artists, who buy houses to rest here and then go back to the city. They have not actually moved to this place, they do not really feel the earth here. However, on the surface, they find this place to be very quiet. This kind of people is only escaping reality. Another kind of people is wholeheartedly fed up with city life. They want to completely change their working and living styles. In the process of doing so, they eventually found it impossible to leave this place. The third kind of people has no idea of what this place should look like. They do not know why they stayed in the city in the first place. They saw other people coming here, so they followed too."

I thought about what Luo Xu was saying. Yes, Yunnan's ancient towns of Dali and Lijiang had become not just artist colonies, but backpacker paradises as well. Both Lijiang and Zhongdian had been embroiled in conflicts over which place was the original Shangri-La, as described in Hilton's novel, *Lost Horizon*. "Should I go to Lijiang, or Zhongdian?" I asked Luo Xu. "Some people say that the real Shangri-La is there. What do you think?"

"Many places claim themselves to be Shangri-La. Lijiang, Zhongdian, Tibet, Qinghai and even certain towns in Sichuan are competing with each other for this name. Sure, all these areas have a connection to Tibetan Buddhism. But the sad irony is, they are competing for this name entirely for commercial objectives, without understanding the concept of what Shangri-La is really all about. In fact, you can find Shangri-La everywhere in the Qinghai-Tibetan Plateau, in every blade of grass. It is not a place that can be designated by any single person. I think Shangri-La is a concept, very natural, peaceful like heaven, a realm of self survival and vital energy, very wild and elemental. This does not mean it can be found in any particular place. To actually find it would be too disappointing. If the author who wrote *Lost Horizon* were to be alive now, he would not tell us that it was ever his intention to find where Shangri-La is really located."

"Then am I taking the correct road to Shangri-La?"

"Most people do not dare go to these places because they are afraid of high altitude sickness. Europeans who came here do not feel comfortable, the Chinese too, though this is their own country. In fact, the Chinese people's lives are getting better now, so they are especially afraid of getting sick. They are afraid that they will step on something and fall, so they are afraid of the possible and most don't dare to go to Zhongdian. In having a better life, they are now afraid of losing what they have. Actually, you should go there. Reaction to high altitude is nothing, maybe a bit of difficulty in breathing, but not as serious as people say."

It was clear that materialism had become the single paramount value of China. While the material West was seeking something spiritual in the East, China had already lost what it had to give. Chinese would not go to Shangri-La for fear that it might cost them their materialism, both literally and spiritually. Pondering this thought, it left me shocked, feeling quite empty and disappointed inside.

"You are from Yunnan originally. When did you first go to Zhongdian?" I was really curious as to when Luo Xu himself first explored Shangri-La.

"My first time to Zhongdian was five years ago, late summer, same season as now. One moment, it rained. Another, it cleared. When I arrived, there was a glimmer of sunlight scattered on top of some small distant hills. Because of the rain, it was not very clear, creating a pattern of strange colors in the sky which is hard to describe. If the lamas saw this, they would think of such colors as a gift from heaven. They would lie down, prostrate themselves and meditate. They respect pure natural beauty very much and express their feelings toward nature with the totality of their emotions. They might stand there nervously, shaking with emotion, even writing poems on the spot. I think at such moments, one's eyes are of no use as communication with nature is already coming directly from one's heart. In such situations, don't bother taking photos. You take a photo, go back and look at it. Then it has no meaning anymore. Why? In such moments, a human being merges with nature. At that very moment, I melted, disappeared, and was digested into that place. This was my first trip to Zhongdian."

"The question then is not 'where' but 'what' Shangri-La is."

"As for finding Shangri-La, I think Zhongdian should be the right place because it has not been torn apart by human beings yet. Such a mysterious concept as Shangri-La cannot lie in a city. At the same time, we cannot use our fingers to point at any single place and say it is Shangri-La. We can only use our hearts to tell us what Shangri-La is. Shangri-La can be found, it lies inside your heart. Everyone can look within himself and find his own Shangri-La."

Luo Xu then led me into one of the beehive catacomb buildings that exhibited his works. The cavernous brick room was round, like an auditorium. On one side were rows and rows of heads which he sculpted from ceramic. Some were laughing, some crying, others screaming; or so they seemed to me. The figures all faced him in rows, one tier upon another, in a half circle, like singers in a choir. "Do you know what I like to do more than anything else in the world?" Luo Xu asked me with a look on his face of forlorn sincerity, or unrepentant intention.

"What?" I asked with curiosity.

Luo Xu pointed to the heads facing us. He then pointed to a CD player in the corner. "I like to play music very loudly in this room; classical music. Then, I would stand in the center before all of these heads I have created and conduct music. I can do this for hours."

On any given day at an undetermined time, Luo Xu will stand

before the heads he had created. They explode with expressions —
some laughing, some crying, others screaming. Luo Xu will then
put the music out loud and wave his hands slowly like a conductor
before a choir. He will conduct for hours. But the heads will remain
silent. On such occasions, his pet donkey will sit there attentively,
and listen. Aside from the donkey, no one listens.

Purple Moon Crying in Rain

Kunming. The old city is now gone. Wood, stone and tile houses have been smashed, obliterated and covered with cement. For some, it is economic progress; for others, the uprooting of their roots. I followed an address San Bao gave me to a nondescript building. I could not remember, but it could have been a factory which had been converted into a school. I was to discover later that it was a half-built theater. I stood outside looking at the cement walls and smudged glass windows. It was raining in the parking lot.

I heard the sound of chanting. It rang through my ears with a piercing sound like a call from wilderness, the cry of a purple moon in rain. It haunted the recesses of my thoughts. The echo reverberated for a time that could not be measured by the sound of breath. I followed the sound up four flights of cement stairs and entered a dance studio. The children stood on both sides of the studio, their tiny bodies draped in traditional clothing of their village. It had been sewn three generations ago, passed from grandmother to mother to daughter. They were proud of their clothes. They were unaware of my presence. They were singing.

I found Yang Liping, China's legendary dance performer, sitting on the floor against a mirrored wall of her studio, her back pressed against it. The singing village girls were reflected in the mirror and in the sunglasses of Yang Liping. Her hair, laced with chunks of turquoise with coral, was braided Tibetan-style, and she wore a red Chinese jacket with the sleeves torn off, their edges frayed. She asked me if I wanted to listen. She indicated before I spoke with her that I should listen to the children sing. This was a prerequisite for my discussion with her. So I sat on the wooden studio floor beside Yang Liping. She said nothing. We listened. The children sang.

When listening to the village voices, one should not sit in a chair. It is best to sit on the floor — legs crossed, squarely and firmly — in touch with the solidity beneath you. I asked Yang Liping about the philosophy of sitting cross-legged on the floor and listening to children sing.

"Regardless of philosophy or art," she explained, "this is related to the lifestyle and environment of Yunnan, which is inseparable from nature and the very basis of life. This is not empty-talk philosophy. Ethnic minorities pray to the sun. This is their philosophy. The sun is fire. They do not know about science. They just know that fire is a necessity of life. They know that they need fire and the sun is fire. If the warmth of your personality is like fire; if your dreams are like fire, they will burn. If your love is like fire burning, you can understand the depth of this rationality through the simple expression of dance."

She pointed to the children dancing, their movement like spring flowers awakening after the rain and autumn leaves blowing in the cool wind. "They must retain the entire composure of their dance," she explained, pointing with long thin white fingernails, spreading

them with her fingers like an unfolding fan. "They use their entire hearts in their dance. This is not a job. It is not an assignment, but an essential necessity. When they are happy, say, upon getting married, they dance. When the old die and they have a funeral, they dance again. When they go to the fields to plant rice seeds, they sing. When they harvest, they sing. Dance, in its essential form, is like this."

"When you were young, was it your intention to become a dancer?" I asked her, pointing to the children dancing and chanting before us.

"I never went to dance school," she confided. "But in the school of life, I have felt and have searched for what life is all about and come to express this. Through this, there is meaning. It is not just putting music on and dancing to it. This has no meaning. I am now in the Central Ethnic Dance Troupe, where my career is, but I do not plan to stay on the stage dancing and singing. I sometimes think about my childhood, dancing alongside the river, in the village, dance is more natural. Now, we must perform as a matter of work. But my composure is still that of before." She pointed to the children chanting, enveloped in village tradition. "Once you have left your roots, you lose it. You will become light without strength, with nothing behind to support you. In the end, you will not even be yourself."

"You yourself are like the children from the village that you now teach. You did not study dancing but have become one of China's greatest modern performing dancers. You even created your own style, your own school of dance. Your Peacock Dance is famous, recognized around the world. How were you able to do this without professional training?"

"Most of mankind depends on their mouths to express their feelings toward nature, toward the things in life around them. Since childhood, my language was dance. If I speak my feelings toward life, you may not understand because I cannot use words to express my feelings. My most direct language is the language of motion. Some people may ask how language can become expressed in dance. I can only explain that I have found the best language for me."

The children continued to sing. They moved like stalks of rice in fields, being blown by a wind that finds its breath in the transition between late summer and early autumn, a time which passes by without being observed. "You must see which angle you view ethnic dance from," Yang Liping continued pointing with her long white fingernails at the girls moving in shuffles across the dance floor. "Natural environment is the basic source of life. This kind of dance, which is associated with the basic elements of life, is inseparable from the ethnic people themselves. You must respect them and know that this is the purest and the most precious of things. It is not my technique in performing the Peacock and Moon dances that has given me acclaim; it is the correct expression of those things of value to a culture. We are not a museum."

I thought about Kunming today, which is unlike the Kunming I knew twenty years ago while wandering through the cobbled, tree-lined streets that wrapped around the wood and stone houses of another century. That is gone forever. I could not find the address of Yang Liping's school because everything in this city looked the same, just blobs of cement. "But if the spirit of a culture is the basis of expression, how can expression retain in art if the culture is in danger of extinction?" I asked.

"With this kind of future, we will lose this kind of natural way of living," Yang Liping sighed, shaking her head. "Because now many ethnic groups do not sing, do not dance and they live in cement buildings covered with bathroom tiles, living a modern lifestyle. They are absorbed by many materialistic hopes. They will lose their original selves, it will be gone. We must work to maintain this. But we cannot organize and force them not to lose this because everyone will want to live a modern life. While they should protect and keep what is theirs, we cannot force them to do this. So the most rational way to do this is to quickly grasp these things which are about to be lost and find a way to keep them. In another one hundred years, the villages will not exist, their people will be gone. They will be the same as ethnic Chinese. Maybe on stage or in a museum, you will be able to see what they were. Maybe in the end, we will only be able to save just this little."

Yang Liping explained how she had been traveling for months to the remotest villages of Yunnan Province searching for traditional songs and dances being performed in their original states. The children she brought back to Kunming as her students were all from these villages, in fact, they were not performers at all, but village children. Their songs and dances were only part of their natural village life.

"They do not have any written language or technique to keep records of their dance or culture," Yang Liping explained. "How your mother teaches you is how you dance or sew. It is entirely an oral tradition. Their music has no fixed foundation. You hear them sing and it sounds so good, all four tones together in harmony. But they have no composed music, no conductor. It is not composed but it comes together as if it is. It is their own natural sound that comes together in a harmony which cannot be composed, because it is their true natural expression. This is the same with their dance. Look at their clothes, it is hand sewn with special thoughts. There is no way to write this down and record it because it is part of their natural life."

"Then these arts are in serious danger of being lost, and soon."

"There are now only a few of these songs and dances. Yunnan is not bad in that because of its poor transportation, and therefore the natural life of its people has been as less affected as other places. It is a border region, a mountain region. There are places where we cannot drive, so we walk. These places are better. But soon they will be gone. The government does not stop developing new roads and it does not stop developing tourism. This creates new influences which changes village life. Young men do not like wearing traditional clothes anymore; they prefer jeans. Moreover, it requires people like me to search and find their traditions and bring them out, to dust off what is there and make it clean again." Yang Liping pointed out that in bringing dances and songs from the villages to her dance school, she was keeping traditions intact, bringing out the best and not engaging in re-choreography. "Somebody has to do this. If there is too much dust covering the beauty of these traditions and they cannot be seen, then we have a responsibility to clean it off and make it clear. It is as if a tree is standing before you. You cannot cut it. You should only trim it to make it look better. Take away the excessive elements and that tree will stand beautifully. It is also natural. It is always there. It is not cross-bred to look good."

"In a way, you are rushing to preserve your own heritage," I asked. "Isn't that what this is all about?"

"In my bones, I respect basic things. When you create a dance, it should naturally accord with the meaning of the dance. Internal meaning and structure of a piece of art must be in harmony with itself. There cannot be a piece of outer skin carrying a lot of unrelated things. I am strongly against this. What is modern? Tell me! It is not just wearing jeans and eating at McDonald's. It is not just using an electronic music synthesizer." She pointed to village girls rehearsing on the floor before us. "You can see their dance is very modern because a modern sense of meaning is implicitly within it. Look at the colors of their clothing. A French fashion designer can only come this far, but cannot exceed what they have. Yes, just because his color design is very modern and fashionable, you cannot dismiss what they have as ethnic and antique. The point is, their intention and ideas are modern. It does not matter what you are wearing. Their music is modern. The problem is, can you understand it? It is not that you say you are modern or you wear something that is modern. Do you have the ability to appreciate their modernity? On stage, you may be looking for modern technology and lighting effect to give colors, which is only an external matter, but do they have modernity within their spirit?

You cannot say that they are backward. This kind of spirit we want to express and let others come to know."

"What does this spirit mean to you?"

"Healthy, composed, beautiful. This is philosophy and art which all mankind can understand. Look at the composer San Bao. His music and style is modern and beautiful. When he came to see my students perform here, he broke into tears. Why? Because he realized this was music in its original purity. He cried because upon hearing them, he discovered the beauty of music and how it moves others. Dance was originally a total expression, not a fulfillment of duty. He has seen too many performances that were for the sake of completing an assignment, for money, for a purpose. But this moved him because it was purely for spirit and the expression of the inner self."

"Yes, San Bao had said that if I come to Yunnan in search of Shangri-La, I must first search you out!"

"When I was a child, my grandmother taught me — of course she did not use the term Shangri-La — that our ethnic group uses the term 'Mo Li Ye Na'. Later, after I grew up, I understood. In fact, the idea is the same. It is a question of differences in language. Westerners call it Shangri-La. Chinese call it a 'Peach Garden Beyond the Realm'. At Lijiang's Jade Dragon Snow Mountain, they talk about a 'third world' Shangri-La. Many young boys and girls are not afraid to die. They actually believe in dying, because it is natural phenomena. Couples will climb the Yulong (Jade Dragon) Snow Mountain and jump off to their death because they are going into the third realm of Yulong, to Shangri-La. When they go to the third realm of Shangri-La, they believe that is the best, so they are not afraid to die. It is an even better place to go to after death. They are the romantics. They are not like others who feel that after death, you become dust, and it is sad. They are not like this. They believe that after a person dies, he will go to the third realm. It is very romantic. It is not that they are not afraid; they are idealistic. Just like Tibetans turning a prayer wheel. After death, they will reincarnate and it will be better. This hope allows them to go through the realities of this world with happiness. Look at the Tibetans. So what if life is somewhat hard? Because the environment they live in is harsh, the air thin? There is a lack of oxygen, and it is freezing cold. It is a difficult place to live in. So you must have hope — your own hope — like Shangri-La. If your hope is built on this, you will not be afraid of death. They are not afraid of the suffering in their lives because the future lives will be better. They live in a dreamlike world, not a clear precise world like yours. You want to find out precisely what and where Shangri-La is, to define it and tell others. But they are in a dream and for them, this dream is Shangri-La."

"You are also a Bai ethnic minority from Dali, right?" I asked. "Some say Dali is Shangri-La. Others say Lijiang or Zhongdian. Regardless, is Shangri-La here in Yunnan? What do you really think?"

"Our ethnic Bai minority believe in every person's soul, so there is a culture of wizardry, communicating with the dead, with the soul. They know there is lots of empty space for communication only in the spiritual, in the ideal. Why are Yunnan's people so gentle? You must ask yourself this question. Here, the environment is so nice — clear water, green mountains, great natural outdoors — so their lifestyle is very happy. They sing and dance and their culture is very rich. They won't get angry and frustrated. In the mountains, you will often see a woman carrying huge bundles of scrap wood, bigger than the woman herself, climbing the mountain trail, twisting threads for spindling busily being sewn in her hands as she walks, with the naturalness with which we might drive and use the mobile telephone. She accepts this and does not have any anger toward this life. She thinks, 'Since I have such a life, I must give birth, have many children and let life multiply.' It is a very natural attitude toward life."

"Then you follow a philosophy of a natural attitude toward life, both in your life and dance. Is that right? The naturalness of your dance is an expression of your philosophy toward life?"

"One must first 'sense' and then 'realize'. Many people have sense, but no realization. For instance, in dance, you can say you studied a lot, you watched a lot, you feel that dance is good, but when you try it yourself, you cannot express yourself, in such a case, there is sensation but no realization. Your body cannot realize expression. You can only feel good, but not express it. Many people have gone to many universities and have lots of knowledge and experience, but they cannot write a good novel. Many students have studied lots of dance, but cannot dance well. To realize or awaken is realization. It is to have the vision to see and then to do it. It is not that you can only see but not do. This affects dance, fashion, and even film. Does that camera focus and capture that particular meaning intended? This is important. Can it completely express it? Ask yourself! Dance is like that. This is something that cannot be taught. It can only be within your own self. If you practice without desire or feeling, then it is useless. If you have desire and feeling, and you have realization, then you can achieve it."

Feeling, comprehension, realization... I wondered to myself, "Maybe then the search for Shangri-La is not about a place but about feeling and comprehension?" I was more confused than enlightened.

"If your intention is to find Shangri-La, but your way is all messed up or if you hurt or kill people on the way, then how can you find Shangri-La? In your heart, there is no Shangri-La. It's only from your mouth that you say you are looking for it. You want to find a happy life, but you do not create that happy life. Don't you realize that a happy life must be created. There are two directions. One is realism, while another is your spirit and attitude. If you think I must definitely find a spiritual Shangri-La and make it a very ideal atmosphere, the result — being what you do — is all messed up. Then that spirit is false. You do not have any belief, so you do not know what Shangri-La is all about. You talk about living happy days, but you don't go out and create a happy life, then you will not be happy. This is the difference between realism and spirituality. If you want to fix Shangri-La at any particular place, then you will lose the meaning of Shangri-La because Shangri-La is not in a location. You cannot use one place or one product to represent Shangri-La. Therefore, Shangri-La cannot be said to be in Zhongdian. It cannot be fixed in Lijiang, not just because Lijiang is beautiful and people say that this could possibly be Shangri-La. The author of that book was searching for a lost Shangri-La. No place can represent Shangri-La. Only spirit can. Lijiang and Zhongdian are Shangri-La. Are they the most beautiful places? They are only places where the natural environment has been quite well protected, so you might think that they are Shangri-La."

"So you are saying that neither Lijiang nor Zhongdian is Shangri-La?" I asked, quite taken back by her words.

"To really find a place is meaningless," she warned, raising one thin white fingernail, unfolding the other delicate fingers, spreading her hand like a white fan. "We can only search for it. We can seek it in what is beautiful. Already from the spiritual perspective, we have found it. In Yunnan, there are many places where you can feel Shangri-La. But to say you can completely find it is impossible. The 'Peach Garden' of Chinese legend does not exist. The movement of dance can achieve a beautiful appearance from dance moves. Because of the effect dance has, you can be affected. Music and clothing might be beautiful, if it is beautiful, then this is Shangri-La. There are writers who have come back and said there is no Shangri-La as it has been destroyed. So they can only go and look further."

So I went to look further. I would follow her directions to see for myself, traveling to Lijiang and then to Zhongdian, the two counties claiming to be Shangri-La. When I left Yang Liping's studio, I could hear lingering voices of village children. They were still singing. As I traveled to Lijiang and Zhongdian, hitchhiking along a network of roads which wound past villages, through valleys and into mountains, I could still hear their echoes clinging to my memory, haunting internal recesses of meditation upon smooth lake waters waiting to be touched. The purity of village children chanting had been captured for a moment and held in Yang Liping's vision, it is a call from the wilderness, the crying of a purple moon in rain. I was reminded to stop for a moment before sacred snow-capped mountains, wait, listening for snow to melt.

Rock Concert in Rain

I arrived at the Jade Dragon Snow Mountain Music Festival. The rock concert had begun and it was already dark. There was no snow, only rain. I could not listen to the snow melt because the music was too loud. The music was being drowned in the rain. It rained throughout the concert but this did not prevent a huge crowd from climbing to the mountain's foot, already 3,000 meters above sea level, to listen to the music. The rain created a special effect, forcing stage lights to split into smithereens of fractured kaleidoscopic lights against the puncturing raindrops that left the performers and audience soaked. I wandered through the crowd, through the music, through the rain. As kids and police danced, the effect was surreal, explaining why so many had come out for the concert despite so much rain.

In the morning, it was sunny and fresh, the feeling of clarity after a rain. I called Kaiser Kuo, one of the first and perhaps the last of China's hardcore rock stars. Founder of legendary rock band Tang Dynasty, he was now heading another band named after another dynasty, Spring and Autumn. We met by a river in the old city of Lijiang for coffee. The river ran past cafés, thus giving the place an air of Venice. The coffee was dark Yunnan. It had that pungent oily smell of Yunnan hillside slopes, cut by hands of ethnic tribes wearing clothes passed down from grandmothers to mothers to daughters, and the smell of rain. I stared into the cup of coffee

looking for Shangri-La. I guess I was not looking hard enough. So I asked Kaiser where l should look next.

"How did your concert go last night?" I asked him

"Extremely well, except for the rain. We were nearly rained out. The whole carpet on the stage was soggy. It felt as if electricity currents were running through me the entire time. It was like having a leaking battery tied to you. But the crowd was really enthusiastic. We were sort of the only band left with long hair. Even though Spring and Autumn is a new group, we still carry the fame of my old band, Tang Dynasty."

"Many are calling this music festival the Woodstock of China. Is it?"

"I do not think it is going to be the seminal defining event in the musical life of a whole generation. But it is a start. People flew in from all over China. There was a huge group from Kunming and another from Sichuan as well. The Beijing rock crowd was also here. There are only a few towns in China that have become centers for rock music. One of these cities is Kunming, another is Chengdu. People fall in love with these towns. There is something really great and cool about these places. Beijing, of course, has always been China's main center for rock and roll. In fact, the entire idea for this music festival was started by Cui Jian, and it's a great start," Kaiser thought for a moment while staring into his coffee cup. "Unfortunately, the big attraction — the snow mountain — could not be seen because of the rain."

"Why is China's music scene drawn to Lijiang to hold a Woodstock-style festival? Will Lijiang become the next rock-and-roll town in China?" I asked. "Is there some kind of search for inspiration in Shangri-La taking place now among China's music circles?"

"Frankly, I am not sure if the Lijiang musical festival itself is the manifestation of this tendency, and I don't think Lijiang is going to become a center of rock. Like other things in China, the Shangri-La idea is a great attraction for the West, which is the whole thing behind this New Age music. There is a sort of mystical Orientalism giving rise to white Buddhism — American Buddhists and European Buddhists. This is something which has its root way back before Hilton's Shangri-La or *Lost Horizon*. The Rosicrucians, for example, was one of the European mystical sects that are fascinated with Tibet. They sought this mystical land, believing that Christ was reincarnated or reborn there. After this Christian infection of Tibet, I am not sure what it is. Many Westerners are crazy about the Himalayas. They really take in this hocus pocus stuff — the jewelry, the chanting music, the *thankas*."

"Is this just an optical illusion of Christianity? Maybe the ideas behind Christ's teachings originally came from Buddha and Christianity just recycled reincarnation as a concept?"

"I am really not going that far. I am not a scholar of religious history, so I do not really know the direction of transmission. In fact, you see a lot of images in Buddhism like Guan Yin or other Bodhisattvas who look very much like Virgin Mary or saints for example. I do not know what is the direction of transmission, whether it is just illusion between Christianity, I cannot see. I see in the West a lot of people who for sound scientific reasons, reject Western traditions, but lose all sense of that when approaching Eastern philosophy. They suddenly embrace anything that comes from the misty East. That is what is sad to me. It is sort of cheap thing, I think, in some ways."

"In a way, we now have the emergence of a 'Shangri-La chic', right?"

"Now in China, you see artistes like 'Dadawa', whose real name is Zhu Zheqin, an ethnic Han musician who has really created something which is right out from the Yunnan-Tibetan Plateau. You can see that young Chinese are now wearing batik clothes and silver jewelry, and listening to New Age music. The sad irony is that much of the value in this culture is coming to China via the West. It is a type of fashion. It was not long ago that you would see Chinese wearing a high mandarin collar, Chinese buttons, lime green — the Shanghai look — until it became popular in the West. What was suddenly running down the catwalk in Milan, Paris, and Tokyo suddenly came back in China in full force, which is an ironic boomerang effect. Likewise, a town like Lijiang suddenly becomes popular again. I hate to use the term 'again', but it is almost Orientalism being re-imported with Eastern people re-embracing their supposed heritage because it became popular in the West for some reason. What you see happening lies in this reason."

I stared into my coffee cup, thinking about what Kaiser was saying. For a moment, I stopped looking for Shangri-La in the coffee cup and instead, asked Kaiser, "Westerners are trying to find Shangri-La through Buddhism, music or fashion. But doesn't the search for Shangri-La go deeper than that?" Coffee, yet to be drunk, was getting cold in the crisp morning air.

"I am not sure," Kaiser thought for a moment, now staring into his coffee cup. "There are many people in the West who are familiar with Shangri-La, even if they have only heard of a utopian place where people do not age. Yes, there are many

people who come here searching for Shangri-La. But in reality, the Westerners and visitors who come here are not really searching for Shangri-La; they are searching for beautiful scenery, ethnic minorities with beautiful costumes, and the gorgeous architecture. The town is absolutely beautiful in spite of what has happened in the past few years with tourists overcrowding the place and becoming like Venice where the river canals are lined with parallel souvenir shops. But the real irony is that most people who come here are still big groups of tourists following some guy holding a yellow flag. They are not going to see the charming little villages. They are going to stay in those white bathroom tile and blue glass hotels. They need infrastructure. They need to sing karaoke. Sure, for experimental experience, you can go and have a Tibetan barley mash with yak meat if you want. But there are always pizzas around. Look, in Dali, there is a 'Foreigners' Street'. It happens everywhere in this region that opens to tourism."

"It is extremely ironic that three counties have been in dispute over who will use the name 'Shangri-La'. There are also three provinces which all want to be known as Shangri-La at the same time," I had already traveled from Tibet, through Qinghai and now, in Yunnan's Lijiang. Soon, I would go to Zhongdian. I was basically making the rounds of all places competing for the title of the "real" Shangri-La. "It's all driven by the material objective of tourist dollars, not any spiritual objective of what Shangri-La is supposed to be."

"Can you have what they call in World Bank lexicon, 'sustainable development', and at the same time, keep the culture?"

"Yes, on one hand, things have changed here dramatically within just a few years. All these quaint little guesthouses now have ADSL Internet access, and the cafés are knocking out banana pancakes and apple pie to backpackers. On the other hand, this is livelihood for the people living here, so there is nothing wrong with Shangri-La business. I would do the same thing if I were they.

The reality for them is that Shangri-La is something that draws Western tourism. To them, it does not have anything to do with their culture."

"Aside from the tourists and backpackers, let's look at the music concert. What are the artistes trying to seek by coming here?"

"The artistes are trying to seek audiences. They are obviously interested in this field, if you walk through any mid-sized American town, you will see the New Age shops with crystal from Atlantis, tarot cards and all that stuff. It personally makes me want to vomit. I've seen this before. One of my friends in Beijing who runs a nice little bar next to Hou Hai always plays a New Age music CD. One day, I took a look at the CD cover and it had a little sticker on it saying 'Wood Protector Mirror', with a little *'Ba-gua'* oriental mirror attached in the middle of it. This is all cheesy Chinese. The names of the songs were like 'Mountain', 'Cloud' and 'River'. I looked at it and there were some Tibetan Buddhist symbols on the cover. Then I noticed the artiste's name is something like Hydrick Vongroomon — a German guy. He is trying to make something out of this New Age chic. It makes me sick."

"Why does it make you sick?"

"Clearly it is just an attempt to milk this New Age trend for whatever it is worth, to grab the people who are looking for some meaning in life. Yes, it's an illusion. Maybe it's not even that. It's a kind of vulnerability which has made them accept, without a real reflection, the mystical eastern philosophy, while rejecting the religious traditions handed on to them by their parents."

"So in a way, Westerners are turning away from Western values, turning to Eastern values and looking for the instant noodle, which is Shangri-La in a package. This in turn calls for the commercializing of Shangri-La in a way, which in the end, may make Shangri-La not so Shangri-La. Is that what's happening?" I thought for a moment about what I had just said, staring into a now almost empty cup of bitter Yunnan coffee. "If so, then what is Shangri-La?"

"It's a fictional notion drummed up by a guy named James Hilton from a book he wrote. It might or might not be predicated on a real physical location, possibly near Zhongdian, Lijiang, or near Dali."

"So it's not an overall concept of Qinghai-Tibetan Plateau culture?"

"No, it's not. I think it's an amalgamation of the very features of that or a Westerner's imagination of what those features should be. Yes, sure, it also includes a repackaging of utopian ideas that have always been around. The Chinese have the idea of an eternal peach blossom garden, or 'Penglai Island'. Qinshihuang, the founding emperor of China, sent a mission of 500 young virgin men and 500 young virgin girls abroad looking for this island. They found Japan instead and stayed there."

"When did Hilton write his book *Lost Horizon*, which introduced the Shangri-La idea?"

"In the 30s, almost 70 years ago, and suddenly, there is a new resurgence of interest in finding Shangri-La, of coming to this region. This is due to a convergence of two things, which are ironically in conflict. China is opening up, wanting tourists' dollars and Westernization. The New Age phenomena in the West seeks to achieve a higher plane of human consciousness in finding and practicing a set of non-materialist Asian values now rejected in Asia, being replaced by Western materialism."

"Then is Shangri-La just an illusion? And as soon as you go and seek it, it disappears?" At this point, I was beginning to become disillusioned.

"Sure. It never existed in the first place, it isn't a real place. There may be some real articles talking about it, but it's a meaningless idea. There are many other places like Kunlun Mountain or Penglai Mountain. Every culture has their own secret places where people never age and everyone is peaceful and happy. Native Americans had a lot of ideas like this. Indian culture has such ideas in South Asia. In European civilization too, we have Thomas Moore, we have Plato's Republic. These are not real places. They are only in your mind. But it never hurts to keep looking."

I had to keep looking. The snows were melting in the rain. They were rushing down a creek in Lijiang, beneath delicate stone bridges, past banana pancake cafés lining old canals twisting along narrow alleyways. A long line of Taiwan tourists were walking on ancient stones, searching in an orderly manner, behind the shadow of a young Beijing gift in a yellow baseball cap carrying a yellow flag. She was leading the tourists to Shangri-La.

Shangri-La in a Cup of Tea

I followed the river, crossed a bridge and lost the yellow flag, which disappeared around a corner of an old stone wall which looked as if it would collapse but would not because it was not at least five centuries old. Stepping up from the street, I walked through the door of a quaint little café filled with Tibetan antiques tucked into the wall of a side street by a river running through Lijiang. "Is this your café?" I asked.

"Yes, this is Dadawa Café," replied Zhu Zheqin, pop star known as "Dadawa" to the world. "And Dadawa Café belongs to everybody as well." She explained. I was offered a cup of tea.

"So, you mean it is for everyone?" I stared into the empty, blue, cracked ceramic tea cup on the table between us. Someone had gone to get hot water.

"Yeah," she replied. "When you look for Dadawa Café, you think you are looking for me, but it belongs to, you know, whoever is looking for it." Tea was poured.

"Dadawa," I asked. "Tell me, where exactly is Shangri-La?" I held the tea cup. It was now warm.

"When I first came here, I think it was in early 1995, people who worked with me were all talking about Tibet, talking about some kind of ideal place. We kept walking, and we kept traveling, wanting to find something else."

"How did the journey begin?"

"Because I was born in Guangzhou, a really noisy city in south China, for me, everything there seemed limited. When I grew up, as a university student, I just felt that life there was boring. Every day, you have one routine — going to work, studying, talking with people, having a drink with friends in a bar — and that's all. We listen to music and we read some books, and this is all life offered me. Then my heart began to fly because when I was a kid, I had something in my mind that just kept growing within me. So after graduating from the university, I started to travel. First, of course, I traveled around Guangdong. My family gave me great support because they knew I had my own world. They could see it in me. When I was a kid, they gave me more freedom. I started to travel around Guangdong and Shandong, then farther away. In 1992, I had a chance to work in a TV festival in Sichuan. I met a composer who had been in Sichuan for many years composing music, and he was greatly interested in Tibetan music and culture. He helped me collect some Tibetan folk songs over many years. After that, we did a song called Yellow Children. It was from that point that we started our journey to Tibet."

"What were you searching for on that journey?"

"We felt kind of lost. We did not know the things before early times, for instance, where we came from. That is the common question for everyone when we were growing up. We just wanted to know where we came from. All things in the world will become just like that in the end, so we just wanted to find it out. I had a heavy feeling for some time when I lived in the city. We stopped believing anymore. I thought everything is not true. This feeling followed me for many years. I just got confused by the faces, the lives around me in a city, I always got confused and I did not know why. So in my heart, I just felt so lost, I wanted to build my own world. First, I started with music and art. Then I began my journey as soon as I grew up. I kept looking and found a totally different experience when I was in southwestern China, because of its culture, the atmosphere, the way people live there. It is all new for me. It really touched my heart."

"Then, you really weren't searching for something?" I queried. My tea cup was half empty. "Rather, you were being called, is that right?"

"Yes, I do believe my heart, my strong sense of feeling that keeps calling me, calling me, calling me. And then I traveled. On the way to every place, I received a simple kind of peace from my heart. And I started to have conversations with the mountains. That is not real for most people. They will call this a laughable experience. But for me, it is really true."

"When you talk with a mountain, what exactly happens? What do you say and what does the mountain say?" I stared into the tea cup, more carefully this time. "I am just moved, deeply moved, and then they can tell me lots of real knowledge of the world of our coming and relationships between people between nature and the world and our lifestyles. Suddenly, I found a new world. And now, if you want me to tell you what Shangri-La is, I have the confidence to tell you I know this."

"What is it?" I asked, leaning over listening intently. A thin flame from a candle melting slowly on the table in front of Dadawa, lighting her face and reflecting gently in her eyes. "Tell me, what is 'Shangri-La'?" A drop of wax dripped upon the Tibetan brass candlestick below. I had a sense of deliberately looking into the flame and the melting candlestick.

"Shangri-La is in people. It is the ideal world of our minds," Dadawa explained, exuding the confidence of someone who has found what she was searching for, but continues searching for what has already been found. That sense of knowing what you are looking for, taking it away once it is found, and then looking for it again. "But it seems that it is not a real world, if you keep going in that way to find the way in your mind, you will make things come true. It is something you think you realize. It is untrue, but if you keep going, that is the true way to go regardless of distance. The real Shangri-La is in you. That is why I am living in this world."

"So how can one find it?"

She blinked as she looked into the flame. "First step, you must have an ideal world in your mind. That is *really* important for people. But the ideal world for each person is different. You have your own mind, your idea, your country. For everyone, this is different. It is our refusal to make all things just like one thing. Everybody can have his own world in his own mind. But this is only the first step, right? Remember, you have to keep going."

"So you kept going, right? Did you find your Shangri-La?"

"Of course," the small café echoed with her enthusiasm. A young Naxi boy came over and poured more tea into the half empty cup. The cup overflowed, dripping tea on the old wooden table between us. It seeped into cracks which had emerged when releasing moisture some time ago, when nobody could remember, maybe before the wood had become a table. "We are living a true world, but it is not our ideal world," she went on. "Every day, every moment, there are lots of things which make you feel upset sometimes. Sometimes, it feels really difficult. Then, you have to choose, to keep going, but sometimes you will find a little shining light, like this candle, just a little shining flame, and then you just keep going. I think there is nothing that will not come true. If you have confidence, if you have a pure heart, everything can come true. I believe in that."

"What about the Jade Dragon Snow Mountain Music Festival where you sang yesterday. Many young people came from all over China. Did they come to the Jade Dragon Snow Mountain for a music festival, or do you think they are searching for something else?"

"I think the reason they come here is to communicate. Because in China, this is the first time we had a really big event in the Jade Dragon Snow Mountain. Young kids always want to find somewhere to express their feelings, so there is something about a music festival which seems similar everywhere. But I think there is still something different here."

"The search for Shangri-La seems to be an international trend. Some call it 'New Age fusion' lifestyle, others a reaction to globalization, maybe anti-globalization values." I drank some tea from the over-filled cup. "What do you think?"

"I think the problem is not globalization. The problem is, we have limited knowledge of how humanity should develop. Everybody can have his own world. I feel my music and my lifestyle are mine. I think everybody knows I am a Chinese, and a singer. But my life is not so similar with the other fashionable artistes. Because I have my own values of life, I do not think I have to follow the fashionable rules. I have my own world and I think as I keep going, the whole world belongs to me. Sometimes, I open it to anyone who wants to listen and through my music, I can communicate love, beliefs and my whole world. Everybody should have his own world. That is really important. That is why you come to earth. You are just a guest here finding the real meaning of life."

I took a sip of tea and watched the leaves unfolding in heat, reflected against the blue ceramic, and thought about what Dadawa had just said. I was still looking for answers. "What about the so-called New Age music? Does this capture the essence of a new fusion lifestyle or this new craving or trend — call it what you want — a search for Shangri-La?"

"I think the problem is here. That is why my music is greatly influenced by traditional, oriental music, religion and culture altogether. We use new technology to synthesize it, but I still must express myself. Likewise, I do not care whether people try to label my music, saying I belong to this type or that type. At first, I think my music is myself and it represents something in my heart. I think my music just expresses something, because it moves freely. We do not have the burden of what kind of music we have to call it. I would like to call my music 'Dadawa music'. I am not New Age; New Age is a kind of background music."

"Some people say that your music speaks out for the environment, for culture, for the preservation of the Qinghai-Tibetan Plateau. At the same time, environment and ethnic lifestyles are in danger of being bulldozed by development. Can we talk about your music in the context of 'sustainable development'?" I took another sip. A single tea leaf spun in concentric circles. I watched the leaf and listened to Dadawa.

"We come from China," she explained. "We express our feeling to the world, including our people. In our culture, we have had really elegant periods in history and very harsh and painful periods as well. Just like someone's scar, you always show it again and again. I am a new generation. Each time, it really hurts me deeply. It makes me really sad. I want to see hope. But it is not our aim. That is what I want to do. I met many people in Yunnan and in Tibet. They can keep their culture and they also have a good life. I love them. I think it is kind of selfish if you want someone to just remain poor, with no medicine or other essential items. I am a modern person. I do not want people to go back 300 years. It is impossible. But we are living here. We have to build our own world. We still have a way to go but we do not have just one way. Computer is one way, but it is just a tool. Because I have traveled a lot here, I love the children and people here. I want them to have a good life. At the same time, they can keep their cultures and traditions. I think it is difficult. They are trying to do that. But it is difficult because you have to have some kind of knowledge and technology to make this happen."

"What is the one thing that has given you inspiration in your search for Shangri-La?"

"I am a human being. I am living here in the world. I love the earth. It is the true experience. I came here and it is the only way. For everybody, Shangri-La is different. For me, in my heart, I have my own Shangri-La. I think it is different."

"What is it for you?"

"It is just an ideal world, but in this ideal world where everything is real, just like my lifestyle. I like music, traveling, reading, sometimes just keeping silent. I believe life is just like floating water, it will keep going. Shangri-La in my life is a pure heart. When you love people, communicate with people. When you feel sad, when you feel happy, it is just pure. You have no conditions. For me, Shangri-La is the real world. Remember the Buddhist saying, 'Share with others'."

I left Dadawa Café, where I had been searching for Shangri-La in a cup of tea which somebody poured but forgot to take notice of. If anyone realized that Shangri-La was somewhere in that cup of tea, that is, if they had the slightest idea that a round blue cracked piece of ceramic tea cup possessed such a powerful uniting force among people as a vision of Shangri-La, would they rush back, empty the tea in a river outside Dadawa Café and look for Shangri-La inside the tea cup?

I think most people would not take the time to actually pay attention to the depth or width or the precise measurement of tea arising from a tea cup after tea is being poured. They would dismiss such observation as merely vapor. Moreover, they would not bother to throw tea in a river and then look for Shangri-La in the tea cup or the river. As Dadawa said, "Life is just like floating water. It will keep going."

So I left Dadawa after drinking the cup of tea and walked down the ancient cobbled streets of Lijiang which wound along the river where tea should have been dumped and dispersed. It was in this process of walking through the narrow, winding stone slab streets of Lijiang that I became aware of the enormous dispersion that can be emitted through this very simple act of throwing out a cup of tea. I began to wander back to Dadawa Café to look for the cup — without the tea — which had been dispersed. Dadawa had already left. The cup was being washed. I realized that, when searching for Shangri-La in a cup of tea, one must look carefully.

Misty Valleys

I left Lijiang in the afternoon. The sun was setting and the shapes of shadows fit in between slabs of stone. They became thin black lines that cut deeply between the rocks like black rivers cutting through canyons over eons of time. One becomes clear that one is only walking across stone slabs, laid cross-wise like a checkerboard in a street by a Naxi stone cutter two hundred years ago. Then he went in the other direction, but was not lost because he had laid the streets and the tiny stone bridges which he would walk upon and cross when he left.

I left the old city of Lijiang, crossed a valley and climbed a hill. Upon reaching the top, I looked back down at the valley. It rested along a river that split in several places, forming creeks like the branch of a tree which has smaller branches. And when the leaves on these branches fall off, they swift in the wind in circles until they come to the valley. Sometimes, they rest upon the water and flow down a river which split in several places, forming creeks like the branch of a tree that has smaller branches. This is the way the valley can be understood, rich with green in many cooling shades and water which nourishes the green. It is important to understand a valley before you have completely passed through it.

In the valley, there was a village. The village houses were quiet in the late afternoon. The Naxi people of the village had come back to their houses. Their animals were tucked into the stables for the evening. The valley with the quiet houses gave a sense of collective cohesion, not dispersion. The people who live in the valley were contented. They did not realize that I was sitting on a hill looking at their valley, moments before I passed through it. From this perspective, one can feel the contentment of living in the valley oozing upward through various shades of late afternoon green, waiting to be forgotten by an orange setting sun.

I was tired and climbed further to the crest of a road which wound past the valley. Now it would be late and the road to Zhongdian long. I hitchhiked until a jeep stopped. It was driven by a Tibetan who spoke good Chinese. He had long hair like a Navaho Indian and wore turquoise around his neck, tucked under an old sweater. He suggested I wear a sweater as the night ahead would become cool when the orange green became blue.

I hopped into the back of his jeep and we climbed into a blue which became darkness. On the side of the mountain road, I could not hear anything except the rush of a great river, the torrent of force pouring from mountain snows below a winding road into valleys of green. I could not see the river, but only hear the power of water pouring from snow-capped ridges across round, obtuse stones. I kept hearing the sound of water rushing through recesses of my memory and I forgot that I had slept across a sequence of hours when the Tibetan woke me, pointing to a large Tibetan house tucked in a valley which breathed dark purple in the early morning hours. This is where I would stay as the journey was completed.

Journey completed? This did not make sense to me for some

reason. I checked into a two-story Tibetan house which had been converted into a guest house and stood on the wooden balcony looking out across a valley of purple moonlight. Feeling cold and evaporated against the release of heat from a cup of yak butter tea, I clasped the cup close to my chest to feel the warmth, observing what appeared to be a white pagoda rising from the crest of a nearby hillside. I was now in Zhongdian, otherwise known by the name "Shangri-La". But had I really found "Shangri-La"? In the morning, as the sun rose, I drank more yak butter tea and climbed the white pagoda.

In his book *Lost Horizon*, James Hilton describes Shangri-La as a valley surrounded by snow-capped mountains, its grasslands dotted with yaks and sheep and different ethnic groups of different religious beliefs living in harmony, with the golden temple pavilions touching the sky. Leaning against the white pagoda, I looked out over the green valley. There were other pagodas in the distance and the temple roofs behind me touched the sky. Ultimately, the search for Shangri-La had brought me here to Zhongdian, now officially known as Shangri-La County after a long, hard dispute with other counties in the Qinghai-Tibetan Plateau region which all claimed to be Shangri-La in anticipation of the tourist dollars. But here, I was in Shangri-La, and I thought for a moment that maybe I had escaped this wild addiction to dollars through my own search for Shangri-La.

I sat at the pagoda and looked out at the valley. Children came to turn prayer wheels. They wore different kinds of Tibetan clothes, in their simplicity, they were a pageant of color. Turning the wheels, for them, was not a religious experience. It was a game. The wheels turned. The children laughed. They surrounded me as I sat there writing. I asked them if this was Shangri-La. They just laughed. I kept writing. Then, when their laughter turned to mountain mist, I looked up. They had already run away.

There are valleys hidden in the mist. You cannot find them because of the mist. You must assure yourself that they are present and waiting to be found. This requires your mind to be centered in situations of dispersion. Some call it belief. Others call it certainty. When the sun rises, the mist departs. The valleys become apparent and real. You may enter the valleys and look for the remaining mist, but then, they will have already scattered.

Follow the tiny creek which follows the contours of the land and of small rocks which have been carried by the creek and left there when its waters continued down the slope. This slope is the home of the woodcutters. They are simple mountain folks who live off the slope. They cut wood and they have no other trades or sources of income. They live in tiny log cabins made of wood they cut. They weave their own clothes, have few possessions, and ask for nothing from anybody. When I came to one of the woodcutters' homes, he offered me fresh warm milk. It was not pasteurized and was pure. It did not come from a carton, cellophane box or prepared formula. It was very fresh and warm. He was fifty-five years old, but looked more like thirty. Strapped on his back was a grandson. Two granddaughters played on the floor. I sat in his log cabin by a red fire and drank the milk, which had been boiled in a thin aluminum pot over the fire. The two girls sat beside me with curious eyes. They watched me drink the warm milk. I asked the woodcutter if he had ever heard of Shangri-La. To my surprise, he answered, "Yes."

"Of course," he explained, "Shangri-La is here."

"Here?"

"Yes, here."

I looked at the log cabin around me. I could see the outside through the cracks and knew that this would be a cold place to live in the winter, even in autumn or spring. The floor was dirt. There were hardly any possessions. A Tibetan dog barked furiously outside, irritated by my presence. The grandchildren stared at me drinking milk. And I realized that in the poverty which this woodcutter found in his surroundings, he was in Shangri-La.

"Don't you want to live in the city?" I asked the woodcutter.

"Why live in the city? The conditions there are not sufficient. Here, I have the mountain. It is mine to live on. I have little in possessions, but a lot here is mine. Look at the mountain. It has snow in winter, colors in autumn, flowers in spring and in summer, I can cut wood. If I want change, I will move to another mountain. What does the city have to offer? Shangri-La is here. This spot is Shangri-La."

Nyima Tsering's words came back to me like a gunshot from the rooftop of Jokhang Temple in Lhasa ringing across the mountains, deserts and plains I had crossed over the weeks behind me, ringing like a proverbial echo through misty valleys of Yunnan, into the recesses of my mind as I sat before this simple woodcutter. "I have money, I have factory, but I am not happy. Even beggars are more relaxed than me," Nyima Tsering had said. I could see his saffron-robed shadow in a blazing Tibetan sun, pointing his finger to heaven, then downwards to the earth as he said, "This is the search for Shangri-La."

Saving Shangri-La

I found Uttara Sarkar Crees of Gyalthang Dzong Eco-tourism Hotel tucked in a valley surrounded by mountains that generated energy of a kind which can only be found in a quiet valley where intrusion is minimal — an occasional Tibetan, tying a *jingfan* prayer flag to a stone on a mountain. It was this sense of oneness with her environment that Uttara projected in her speech and movement. She was now dedicating her entire existence to developing eco-tourism in the Qinghai-Tibetan Plateau area, sharing her decades of experience with the local government officials in an attempt to change people's thinking, it was her goal to create awareness for what they had and should keep.

"I am from India. I grew up in Africa and lived in Africa and India," she explained, pouring a cup of Indian ginger tea. "Then I was living in Nepal, operating an eco-tourism consultancy. I traveled all around the Himalayas right from Karachi to western Tibet. I never stopped for a rest. In 1987, I was invited by a Tibetan friend to Shangri-La. At that time, I lived for two months and just loved it. After 1987, I wanted to come back here because it was just so wonderful. As I was saying, I had seen the entire Himalayas all over, but I had not seen such beauty as I found here. It fascinated me and I wanted to come back and explore more. Eventually, in the early 1990s, my husband and I came back and received a wonderful welcome from the government here. Anything we wanted to do was fine. And of course, my interest was eco-tourism, so we decided to set up a traditional hotel here that would offer Tibetan hospitality, and started an eco-tourism operation."

"Eco-tourism?" I had heard this term many times. Clearly it was in vogue. "Can you tell me what that really means?" I began looking into the cup of ginger tea, convinced this time that Shangri-La must be somewhere inside.

"It is culturally and environmentally-sensitive tourism. And tourism that can establish certain management standards in relation with places in order to protect the culture and environmental aspects of that area. It also must be sustainable. These are basically the general principles that we follow in developing eco-tourism."

The principles were simple but clear. In fact, eco-tourism does not involve all of the complicated management models of the tourist industry which you need to go to tourism management school to learn and require years in the hotel industry to acquire such skills of management. Rather, eco-tourism is a concept that requires a common sense, something most people lose when they go to management school. It also requires establishing a philosophical platform for one's lifestyle and then living it. "How is the eco-tourism concept going down in China? Is it received well here in Yunnan?"

"I think it took time but they are now very receptive. In China, vast numbers of people travel. They travel together in very big groups. That is what they think is good tourism. But it will take time to slowly understand the fact that tourism creates impact. It brings bad things as well as good things. If a management is put into a place for the purpose of meeting the impact, then we are on our way to developing good quality tourism."

"But by encouraging tourism into an area like Shangri-La, won't it in the end endanger what we have? Maybe those searching for Shangri-La will come here and find the opposite of what they were looking for, because so many people would have come before them."

"Absolutely, there is a very real danger of that. You see, here in this grassland right in front of the hotel, we have at least sixty different varieties of wild flowers, if you were here at the end of May to the third week of June, you would not believe how many wild flowers there are here. We had many botanic groups visiting and they spent days here, all impressed by the number of flowers. We have also very rare flowers too. If you can imagine, in a place like Bika Lake and Shudo Lake, where hundreds of people are beginning to visit all over each year, flowers will become lesser. This is the point of eco-tourism as a concept. You must have the guidelines in place so that the flowers and trees remain protected. There is no damage, or at least, minimum damage to the environment that can be reversed. Otherwise, the very thing that guests come to see will be gone in five to ten years. And the big problem with huge tourism is garbage. People throw their cola bottles out of buses; instant noodle packages are thrown wherever they go. So there have to be guidelines and education in place to keep Shangri-La."

"But the local government is opening up this region to tourism," I said, feeling the warmth of ginger tea emanating across the field of wild flowers we were sitting among. "They are quite excited about the prospects, more flights and all that."

"So far, we only have very few direct flights. There are two flights out of Kunming, one flight a week out of Chengdu, and one flight a week out of Lhasa. It is not the huge number of tourists you see at other sites in China that are very popular. The point is, ten people who are educated or who are sensitive will create less impact than one who is not. There are people who throw trash every place they go. They will take their picnic lunches and leave everything behind. That will infect the environment."

"How do you disinfect the increasing effect of more tourism?" I asked.

"There are tourists who will barge into local homes, which is disrespectful, and buy everything they see. So education for visitors is very important. Here, we have guidelines for visitors to follow and we teach our guides to ensure that these guidelines are followed. Hopefully, the next step will be to educate the drivers who are often with the tourists — but without the guides — to not throw things out of the buses but leave them in the car. I will dispose of them properly. Very simple management is needed but there must be widespread education across the tourism industry."

"What is it that has kept you here in Shangri-La? You have lived in so many beautiful parts of the Himalayas, but in the end, came here to stay. Why?"

"To be completely truthful, I used to suffer from asthma. But since I have come here, I am very healthy. I don't take any medicine. I am both mentally and physically healthy here. People are just wonderful here and they are so hospitable. If you go out in the grasslands and you pass by the tent of a family, even if they have a little bit of cheese, they will share it with you. This great spirit of giving here is what I really appreciate."

"So it is the spirit of giving of the Tibetan people that keeps you here in Shangri-La?"

"Partly that and also because of the way people live here. The religion here and the region itself — the entire area — are spectacularly beautiful, if you look out at the mountains in the back, you will see the blue poppy, a famous flower which explorers, for years, had been looking for." She pointed to a mountain behind the hotel, covered in blue flowers. Strings of *jingfan* were strung across the rocks, indicating a point of spiritual power between the two peaks, where a passage of energy flows between the faces of the two rock surfaces.

"When I first came here, I was so charmed by the people and the region. If Zhongdian is called Shangri-La, I think it is true because it is the gateway to Shangri-La. Beyond here, you travel north toward central and eastern Tibet. They could all be called Shangri-La because they are special, in terms of both scenic beauty and architecture."

"Can Shangri-La be protected? Can eco-tourism really play the role you envision and set a pattern for sustainable development?"

"I believe it takes a lot of work. Small organizations such as ours have to be aware and through practice, set an example as there is a ripple effect. We try to educate people who come in contact with us. When we are trekking, we go on foot on journeys through many villages and communities, where we will stay with them and work with them. Slowly, there will be a way to influence them. Certainly in garbage management, we are showing them, teaching them values and how to protect what they have. But for more practical and quick results, it is important that institutions involved in tourism — hotels, travel companies, tour operators, guides — be educated on what good tourism is. That is the only way to keep the culture and environment here safe. Here, the tourism department is very open-minded. Our governors are amazing. We talked about the problem of garbage and of plastic bags in the valley. As of April, there will be a fine for anybody caught carrying a plastic bag. There are also major efforts being made to take down the tiles from the buildings, giving them a facelift and redecorating them in a style in line with the Tibet character."

I was really amazed to hear this. Virtually every small city and town in China has the same faceless buildings without character and covered in bathroom tiles and blue glass. It is believed that this gives the city a modern look because bathroom tiles are easy to clean. The problem is, nobody bothers to clean them. Here in Shangri-La, the government was actually going against the national trend, chipping away bathroom tiles on buildings and giving them a Tibetan architecture facelift. For China, a real revolution in city planning and aesthetics was finally in the works. "That is happening right now, led by the governor," Uttara emphasized. "It is amazing. This is one of those things you want to do in eco-tourism, to protect the architecture and uniqueness of each area."

"So eco-tourism encompasses not just nature, but culture as well. It is not just the protection of a natural environment but the uniqueness of architectural heritage, the traditions and uniqueness of a region. Is my understanding correct?"

"Yes, but only partially. We have to find ways of protecting the bio-diversity, leaving it as natural and as wild as possible. We have a natural reserve with a whole range of mountains at the base in which we have local ethnic villages. The entire mountains are treasures of wild flowers and plants. There are some very tiny plants which are gradually disappearing from other parts of the earth."

"How does eco-tourism fit in, and how can it save these regions?"

"There is an effort in helping two of the villages earn from tourism and protect the area. They have to protect the area because it is their own land and also because it is their secret mountain where they pray at their secret lake. So there is an eco-tourism project that brings as much income as possible to the local communities so as to allow them to preserve and sustain both their environment and lifestyle. They, in turn, will conserve their own land. But we fear big developers coming in. They are now talking about one developer taking over 50 square kilometers to set up an entertainment park. That is exactly what should not happen here. That will change Shangri-La."

"An entertainment park," I was aghast at the idea. "Why do they need an entertainment park in Shangri-La? They have such crass developments everywhere in China. Can't they leave Shangri-La alone?"

"Very much so," Uttara shook her head in frustration. "That is a trend all over China, where big developers go into a newly opened area. It is happening in Lijiang. It is happening in other areas of Yunnan. It is happening in other cultural heritage areas of China as well. They come in and their concept of tourism may be building an entertainment park. There are hundreds of entertainment parks all over China. I do not see why one needs to have one here. The important thing is what is unique here. As important as what is unique of Lijiang, or unique in Dali, each one has its own uniqueness. Here, our uniqueness is that we are in a region which is one of only two hundred high bio-diversity zones in the world."

"Village people are very simple," Uttara explained. "Through our eco-tourism work, we help them to understand what they have. We do this using a story. There is a story about two frogs in a bowl of yak's cream. One frog tries to jump out, but finds the cream too troublesome to handle, so he accepts his fate and dies. The second frog never gives up. He jumps and tries to get out. Through his jumping, the cream churns into yak butter. Finally, he is free of the cream and he can jump out. I think that is the moral for survival of eco-tourism here. All of us who believe in sustainable eco-tourism must try to keep fighting against the big forces. You must keep trying."

Surrounding her hotel are two protector mountains of the valley. It is believed that luck flows into the shoulder between the two mountains. "Yes, we rebuilt the stupa that was built by our local partner's great grandfather," she explained. Rebuilding the pagoda was the first thing she did before building the hotel. "And every year, the staff of our hotel print prayer flags and hang them between the two mountains over the shoulder. The energy flows between the two shoulders," she pointed to the energy.

Flowers in the Rain

"Om Mani Bemi Hom" is a Tibetan mantra, which asks for peace on the road from which we have come and for peace on the road which we will travel, but have not yet traveled, but dream of traveling one day. The words are carved in Tibetan language upon soft black stones collected from a river in Shangri-La. They are selected from the river by Tibetans passing through this place. They find the stones when they cross the river. They cross the river in search of a place. Nobody seems to know where this place is. You can only find it by crossing the river.

The sacred words "Om Mani Bemi Hom" are carved carefully on the stones, which come in different shapes and sizes, as they are picked from the river. After carefully carving the sacred words, the stones are laid upon other stones placed by others who have come this way before. Eventually, the stones become altars, called *manidui*. They cross the river in search of a place where there are many *maniduis*.

There is a valley of legend, where there are many *maniduis*, one followed by another, stretching as far as the imagination can unravel, into forests where nobody goes, encircling a hill covered with *jingfan* prayer flags, which in itself, is a great *manidui*. If you ask Tibetans in Shangri-La where such a place is located, they either pretend not to know or inform you quietly that you cannot find it. If you ask others, they will think that you have lost your mind. So in searching for the *manidui*, you will save time by not asking any questions at all.

If you travel through a forgotten valley which nobody really knows and the Tibetans will not speak of, you will find horses grazing on wild flowers in the sun. There are rivers which cut through the grasslands, thin rivers and maybe creeks which twist and turn like the knots of a rope, and continue from where they have left, leading to where you want to go, but not telling you how to get there. You can watch them and listen to the sound of water passing through your mind. Light reflected upon patterns of water left by rain in fields that are overgrown with grass and flowers will give you a light feeling and for a moment, you will not be able to walk any further. You may become dizzy. This is neither caused by altitude nor excessive sunlight. It is a process of decomposition of your thoughts. They are disintegrating before you.

Pass through a village. The Tibetans there do not want to be bothered with such questions as directions. They have seen people come and go before. They may ignore you for some time. After persistent questioning, they may listen to your questions, and nod, but they will not tell you what you want to hear. If you leave the village disillusioned, you may stop, sit, and watch horses graze on wild flowers. At this point, you will begin to lose connection with your rationality, which always tells you not to go further. You should now go further.

Begin to look for the place where the stones have been placed. This will appear at a place where split bamboo are fit together as

an open conduct, leading water from a clear mountain stream to a point where water drips from the edge of split bamboo into a small clear pond. Many have drunk from this water and cleansed their hands in an act of purifying the mind. Such places indicate sacred ground. Now start to look for the stones carefully. They have been placed in random locations.

This is the place of many *maniduis*. They begin here, formed of soft black stones from the river with the mantra "Om Mani Bemi Hom" carved upon them, piled carefully to form a *manidui*. Each *manidui* is made from these carved mantra stones. There is an entire row of *maniduis*, one after another, as far as one can see running forests along a trail which nobody follows, covered with giant mushrooms because nobody has treaded here for a long time. The trail of endless *maniduis* runs to a hill decorated with *jingfan* by people who have come and left. It is a sacred hill forgotten by most and remembered by few, where *jingfans* blow in the breeze, sending their prayers to all those who remembered to hang them upon this hill. I stumbled upon this hill entirely by accident after passing by many *maniduis*. Nobody told me it was there. But I had heard that there was such a place waiting to be found because it had been left by others who did not stay long enough to remember its exact whereabouts.

Around the year 1660, Da Bao Fang, the highest-ranking lama of the White Sect of Buddhism, rode on the back of a spirit ram and founded the Da Bao Temple here. In that year, some twenty thousand Tibetans came to lay *jingfan* on the *manidui*. This is an abandoned place. However, Tibetans often return to tie *jingfan* on the shrine hidden atop a mountain of stone, a great *manidui* surrounded by hundreds of *maniduis*, hidden in forest, behind streams and some pastures. It is not always clear when and how the Tibetans get there. They all arrive together to tie *jingfan* on the *manidui*. And together, they leave.

Today, the place is surrounded by sacred goats — maybe the descendants of the sacred ram — upon which the highest-ranking lama of the White Sect rode, or maybe not. They have twisted horns that grow in abstract shapes, unlike the normal rams. Some wear tassels like jewelry in their ears and some had them tied to their mane. The rams have eyes that speak to you very clearly and you can understand their thoughts just by looking into their eyes. So when arriving at Da Bao Temple, you should spend time talking with the rams, just by looking into their eyes.

I climbed the great stupa, a great *manidui*, a small sacred mountain of prayer stones. At each step of the way, there was a Tibetan prayer wheel. I stopped before each one to turn it clockwise.

Upon reaching this place, covered by flickering shadows of thousands of *jingfan* prayer flags carrying wind, I suddenly remembered my life as a little boy, running outdoors, discovering my shadow. This is such a simple discovery — a shadow. But when I chased the shadow, it ran away. When I ran from the shadow, it ran after me. When I turned away from it, it was not there. The shadow was a mystery. I ran in circles creasing it, only to find that when crossing the sun in the opposite direction, it was chasing me. How could such a thing happen? I had wondered, but could not understand.

Maybe we are all chasing our shadows without knowing it throughout a lifetime, but not facing the fact because our shadows are always following us when we are least aware, disappearing when we look for them, sleeping when the sun sets and awaking when the sun rises. Maybe we have not been able to understand the nature of our own shadows this entire time, during an entire lifetime. Then when we die, do our shadows die as well?

I suddenly became aware of this question when sitting in the shadows of thousands of *jingfans* fluttering in the breeze. They were left behind by others whose shadows had come to this place but passed. They had forgotten to remain but had remembered to leave a *jingfan* as a prayer to spread its message in the wind, which might carry the prayer away when lightly touching the *jingfan*, mixing the prayers with shadows of others who had passed when nobody remembered to come here anymore. The tying of *jingfan* requires intention.

I thought about this when my own shadow of silence was interrupted by the screaming of a chicken. Chickens crying in the wind, which touched the prayer flags, were neither prayers nor cries. The chickens were everywhere. They scratched the dirt on the ground and walked around in circles. The stone steps leading to an altar covered in prayer flags, rising in deference to the sacredness of this place and touching the clouds in the sky,

were actually littered with chickens walking in circles screaming. I could not write this because the chickens were making too much noise. Then it began to rain. The chickens got wet and so did I. So I decided to leave and look for the temple near this great *manidui*, which might give me some refuge from the rain and the screeching of wet chickens.

The monks were sympathetic. They do not like the chickens either, especially when they are wet because they will scream in the rain. In such circumstances, the monks can neither sleep nor meditate. So they closed the crumbling wooden doors upon the chickens and let me sit with the goats. These were sacred goats. So I sat for a while on the wooden steps, just out of the rain, talking to the sacred goats. They stared back at me and said nothing. I knew they were sacred because I could look into their eyes and talk to them as the monks were too busy meditating to talk to me. They were eyes that had seen many *jingfans* in a kaleidoscope of colors, which left the impression that life was passing by like wind in the rain. Maybe they were waiting for the *jingfan* to dry in the wind after the rain. I stared at the eyes of a goat and asked why it was raining so hard. He stared back and said nothing. I decided it was time to sit in the rain.

The monks were disturbed by this idea and asked me to stop sitting in the rain but to listen to it pouring on the roof of the temple across the thin piece of bamboo, precariously balanced and sewed as drainage pipe, pouring onto a black stone in the center of the courtyard outside the temple where the goats sat watching my every movement with fascination. They were fascinated probably because I was the first person who was able to stop the monks from meditating. Now we all sat around the wooden steps of the courtyard of this broken-down wooden temple. Me, the monks and the goats — all watching the rain together. It poured.

It rained. Water poured. Drops of rain poured, it was the sound of water striking a bucket. Water fell and struck the bucket. The sound of water in a bucket is the sound of water in a bucket, that is, until the bucket is removed. Then water falls upon stone under the bucket which has been removed. Water on stone smoothens the stone due to the effect of water on stones. Black stone, cold water. Cold stone, black water. Cold black stone and water, water turns the stone black cold and cold black water turns the stone black because black cold water stone becomes what it is from cold black rain dripping on stone. The rain drips cold water on stone which becomes black stone from cold black water.

The water poured out of the bamboo make-shift drain pipe, letting water pour on the black stone in the courtyard of this rundown wooden temple. I remembered hearing as a kid that *kung-fu* monks trained to be masters by sitting under dripping water while meditating. Then I decided to do this by sitting on the black stone with rain dripping off the bamboo drainage pipe on to my head, instead of the black stone. The monks tried to stop me, fearing that I would get pneumonia in the coolness of late Yunnan mountain summer. The sacred goats watched with fascination. They said nothing at all.

I ended up back at Uttara's eco-tourism lodge in a warm room by a fireplace, sitting on Tibetan carpets, drinking yak butter tea. The monks had sent me back after I got soaked in the rain, fearing I would get pneumonia, it felt warm after an afternoon of sitting in the rain with monks and goats, trying to think about meditating with water dripping on my head in the mountain coolness of a late Yunnan summer. Clouds had passed. With them, rain. It was midnight. Guests had gone to bed. The lodge was silent. The flowers on grasslands spreading from the front door of this lodge into the valley wrapped in night were asleep.

I sat there with my yak butter tea and drank it. I was thinking about the sleeping flowers after the rain. The cup was very warm. It was still half-full. I stared at my shadow reflected against a candle flame, flickering lightly upon the flat surface of the yak butter tea, held in stillness. I was searching for Shangri-La, but I was only staring at my shadow. This time, I remembered, when searching for Shangri-La in a cup of tea, to search carefully. For the first time, I was searching without searching.

I was thinking about the sleeping flowers after the rain.

After Shangri-La

In 1933 when James Hilton wrote the classic *Lost Horizon*, he probably never expected to leave generations asking the question: "Where is Shangri-La?" Or that his book would ignite a tourism dispute in western China over which region could call itself Shangri-La for tourist dollars, simultaneously sparking an alternative scene for China's art and culture circles searching for creative space. But believe it or not, that's exactly what happened.

It's amazing how a cup of café latte or yak butter tea can spark new ideas. A coffee chat with Ai Jing became a multi-media project documenting through film, music and writing what could best be described as China's alternative philosophy movement in western China. Music composer San Bao and hip alternative film director Yang Tao joined me, together creating the production of "Searching for Shangri-La", now in its second year.

Our journey through some of the most environmentally sound regions left in the world — Tibet, Qinghai and Yunnan — interviewing artists, dancers, musicians, pop singers, fashion designers, writers, rock bands, environmental activists, monks running grassroots aid projects, several Living Buddha, nomads and ethnic minorities determined to hold on to their traditions. These individuals would change the way I think about China and about the notion of Shangri-La. I learned from these free, creative seekers — inspired by this region or working to save it — that

Shangri-La to them is not just a place, but a vision.

In answer to Hilton's riddle, Shangri-La, a place can be found in China anywhere in the Qinghai-Tibetan Plateau or regions exuding values of this culture, regions sacred to the ethnic minorities inhabiting them, whose lifestyle protects still uncontaminated parts of our eco-system. The tragedy is Shangri-La may be lost very soon.

Therefore to those people, I must make a plea on behalf of myself, the Tibetans, the Muslims, the Buddhist lamas, and the monks whose lives are yet untouched by development and corruption and whose environment is yet uncontaminated, and on behalf of all of those people who will not in their lifetime have the opportunity to visit Shangri-La but to whom it is a vision, a dream, a hope of something better to look forward to, yet unattained, to better protect Shangri-La.

In *Searching for Shangri-La*, we sought to document the "lost horizon", before it is lost.

Laurence J. Brahm

Zhongdian, Yunnan, 2003

北京版权局著作权合同登记
图字 01-2008-1823
Searching for Shangri-La
by Laurence J. Brahm
Copyright © 2006, Marshall Cavendish International (Asia) Pte Ltd.
本书大陆英文影印版由马歇尔·卡文迪什国际（亚洲）私人有限公司授权出版。
This edition is published by New World Press, Beijing, China, under licence from
Marshall Cavendish International (Asia) Pte Ltd and for sale only in China.

图书在版编目（CIP）数据

寻找香格里拉 = Searching for Shangri-La：Off the Beaten Track in Western China：
英文 ／（美）龙安志（Brahm,L.J.）著
北京：新世界出版社，2008. 5
ISBN 978-7-80228-586-6

I. 寻…　II. 龙…　III. 游记－作品集－美国－现代－英文
IV .I712.65

中国版本图书馆 CIP 数据核字（2008）第 049066 号

Searching for Shangri-La
寻找香格里拉

作　　者：龙安志
摄　　影：窦　炎　冀晓明　龙安志
策　　划：黄友义　张海鸥
责任编辑：李淑娟
英文审定：徐明强
英文校对：张民捷
封面设计：贺玉婷
版式设计：清鑫工作室
责任印制：李一鸣　黄厚清
出版发行：新世界出版社
社　　址：北京市西城区百万庄路 24 号（100037）
总编室电话：＋86 10 6899 5424　68326679（传真）
发行部电话：＋86 10 6899 5968　68998705（传真）
本社中文网址：hhtp://www.nwp.cn
本社英文网址：hhtp://www.newworld-press.com
本社电子信箱：nwpcn@public.bta.net.cn
版权部电子信箱：frank@nwp.com.cn
版权部电话：＋86 10 6899 6306
印　　刷：北京外文印刷厂
经　　销：新华书店
开　　本：880×1230　1/32
字　　数：80 千字　　印张：7.25
版　　次：2008 年 6 月第 1 版　　2008 年 6 月北京第 1 次印刷
书　　号：ISBN 978-7-80228-586-6
定　　价：58.00 元

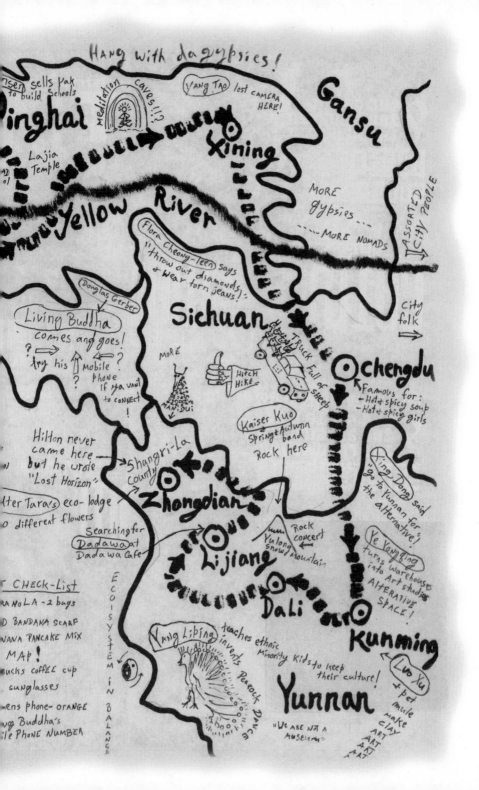

WINDOW TO CHINA